GW00761546

SPORTS

WHITE STAR PUBLISHERS

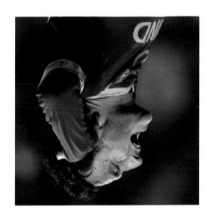

PROJECT EDITOR

VALERIA MANFERTO DE FABIANIS

text

ELIO TRIFARI

graphic design

CLARA ZANOTTI

graphic layout

STEFANIA COSTANZO

editorial coordination

GIADA FRANCIA

© 2010 EDIZIONI WHITE STAR S.R.L.
VIA CANDIDO SASSONE, 24
13100 VERCELLI - ITALY
WWW.WHITESTAR.IT

• Haka, the All Blacks' confrontational pre-match challenge.

ISBN 978-88-544-0539-4

1 2 3 4 5 6 14 13 12 11 10

Printed in Indonesia

CONTENTS

SPORTS

1 • Roma's Francesco Totti celebrates a goal against Inter.

2-3 • Start of the semifinal of the women's 100 meters at the 2008 Beijing Olympics.

4-5 • Prada bowman Bernard Labro submerged by a wave in Auckland on February 5, 2009.

6-7 • Switzerland's Didier Cuche tackles a gate at Beaver Creek in Canada on February 5, 2008. He finished sixth.

8-9 • Australian Felicity Galvez pulls away to win the 100-meter butterfly.

13 • US golfer Tiger Woods celebrates a birdie.

14-15 • Mark Cavendish, holds off Tom Boonen to win the fourth stage of the 2009 Tour of California.

16-17 • Valentino Rossi (46), on the tail of Australian Casey Stoner at the Japanese Grand Prix in Motegi on September 28, 2008.

18-19 • Lolo Jones' shows her disappointment after the final of the 100 meters at the 2008 Beijing Games.

Introduction

Sport has taken a circular route from rite to record and back to rite again as it has developed and seeped into the fabric of civilization. Since people hauled themselves up onto their hind legs and began to create the first communities, they have practiced a number basic sports such as running toward something or to escape a danger; leaping and jumping to overcome natural or artificial obstacles; and throwing objects to capture prey or threaten an enemy. These basic sporting activities include fighting an opponent sometimes with sharpened or otherwise offensive weapons; archery and

• A backhand by Russia's Maria Sharapova at the 2008 Australian Open.

Introduction

STONE THROWING; SWIMMING; DIVING; AND SAILING. AS THE EARLIEST ACCOUNTS SHOW, ALL THESE ACTIVITIES DATE BACK TO THE DAWN OF CIVILIZATION.

IN ITS ORIGINS SPORT THUS TRANSPOSED THE NORMAL ACTIONS OF EVERYDAY LIFE INTO ANOTHER ARENA WHERE THE AIM WAS TO VANQUISH ONE'S OPPONENT NON-VIOLENTLY, NOT TRYING TO BULLY HIM INTO SUB-MISSION, BUT SUMMONING UP ONE'S BEST QUALITIES IN ORDER TO WIN. SPORT IS THEREFORE THE USE OF COM-MON DAILY ACTIVITIES FOR AN ALTOGETHER DIFFERENT PURPOSE. ITS BIRTH AND INITIAL CONSOLIDATION AS AN ORDINARY PART OF COMMUNITY LIFE CAME CONTERMI-NOUSLY WITH CELEBRATIONS, RITES, AND SPECIAL AN-NUAL EVENTS. THE SPRING FESTIVAL OR THE SUMMER

Introduction

SOLSTICE, THE HARVEST OR ESCAPES FROM NATURAL DISASTERS BECAME OCCASIONS FOR PROPITIATORY OR CELEBRATORY RITES OF WHICH SPORT IS A FUNDAMENTAL COMPONENT. SPORT ITSELF BECAME PART OF THE RITE AT FUNERAL GAMES, CELEBRATIONS OF THE BIRTH OF A ROYAL CHILD, OR PERIODIC HOMAGE TO THE COMMUNITY'S DIVINITIES AND LEADERS.

WITH COMPETITIVE OR COLLECTIVE SPORTS ACTIVITIES BEING USED TO MARK PARTICULAR EVENTS, NATURALLY ENOUGH THESE SPORTS EVENTS BECAME SIGNIFICANT IN THEMSELVES.

PROGRESSIVELY, OVER THE CENTURIES, SPORT CHANGED FROM BEING A BASIC ELEMENT OF A RITE INTO SOMETHING WITH AN AUTONOMOUS LIFE OF ITS OWN, AN OC-

Introduction

CASION WHEN THE COMMUNITY OR ITS VARIOUS SOCIAL AND POLITICAL STRUCTURES CAME TOGETHER. FROM HAVING BEEN MERELY A SUPPORT IT BECAME AN END. THE STRIVING FOR EXCELLENCE, FOR SUCCESS, FOR FIRST PLACE, ALSO CHANGED THE VERY NATURE OF SPORT. THE 'RECORD' IS NOT JUST THE FINAL ACT OF A SPORTING EVENT, BUT IS ITS PINNACLE. IT REPRESENTS THE VICTORY OF AN INDIVIDUAL, A SCHOOL, A CIVILIZA-TION, AND, WHEN SPORT WAS REBORN AFTER THE LONG MEDIEVAL PERIOD, EVEN THE CONSECRATION OF A SO-CIAL CLASS, OF A WAY OF LIVING AND ORGANIZING SO-CIAL RELATIONSHIPS. WINNING WAS NOT JUST AN ACHIEVEMENT IN ITSELF, BUT ALSO AN AFFIRMATION OF THE VALUE OF A PARTICULAR WAY OF LIFE, GOVERN-

Introduction

MENT, AND LEADERSHIP. IT IS NOT JUST THAT SETTING A RECORD IS SPORT'S RAISON D'ÊTRE AND GOAL, BUT IT IS ALSO THE AIM OF ALL THOSE WHO PROMOTE AND SUPPORT IT.

COMPETITION AND COMPETITIVE VICTORY THEREFORE BECOMES AN OBLIGATORY MEANS OF DEMONSTRATING THE WORTH OF A WAY OF LIFE. THIS IS WHAT IT WAS LIKE AT THE GREAT GREEK GAMES AT THE TEMPLE OF OLYMPIA AND HOW IT DEVELOPED AGAIN WHEN PIERRE DE FRÉDY, BARON DE COUBERTIN, A FRENCHMAN, REVIVED THE GAMES IN 1894 AND THE ERA OF SUPRANATIONAL, CONTINENTAL OR WORLD CHAMPIONSHIPS BEGAN. POPULAR PARTICIPATION IN SPORTS ACTIVITIES NOW BECAME AN INTEGRAL PART OF SOCIAL LIFE.

Introduction

AS PEOPLE BECAME MORE AWARE OF SPORT'S ROLE ITS MEANING ALSO CHANGED.

THE FRENCH MEDIEVAL WORD FROM WHICH IT DERIVES, DESPORT, ORIGINALLY MEANT THE PHYSICAL MOVEMENT OF OBJECTS NECESSARY FOR SPORTS PRACTICE. HOWEVER THE BRITISH INTERPRETED IT AS A SPORT, THE ITALIANS TRANSLATED IT AS RECREATION, FUN OR ENTERTAINMENT, AND EVERYONE THE WORLD OVER NOW KNOWS IT SIMPLY AND SOLELY AS SPORT. ITS DEFINITION HAS EXPANDED TO INCLUDE ALMOST ALL ORGANIZED PHYSICAL ACTIVITIES, FROM THOSE PRACTICED AT VERY HIGHEST LEVEL TO SIMPLE KEEP-FIT. IT THEREFORE INCLUDES ALL PHYSICAL PASTIMES. SPORT IS NOW A GLOBAL PHENOMENON INVOLVING AND INFLUENCING

Introduction

POWER, INDUSTRIAL AND SOCIAL INTERESTS.

THIS IS WHERE THE CIRCLE HAS NOW CLOSED: THE RITE THAT BECAME A RECORD IS LARGELY A RITE AGAIN. ORGANIZED SPORT HAS BECOME A RITUAL ELEMENT IN THAT, VIA PERIODIC GAMES AND DUE TO ITS OWN PENETRATION INTO THE FABRIC OF SOCIETY, IT CELEBRATES ITSELF. IT IS ITS OWN RITE. THE OLYMPIC GAMES, FOOTBALL'S WORLD CUP OR THE FORMULA 1 CHAMPIONSHIP ARE ALL RITUAL EVENTS, WHICH HAVE LOST ANY CONNECTION THEY MAY HAVE HAD WITH THE RITES THAT GENERATED THEM.

SPORT STILL INVOLVES THAT SAME STRIVING FOR SUCCESS, BUT IT IS A RITE THAT RENEWS, REPEATS AND PERPETUATES ITSELF. THE PICTURES IN THIS BOOK CONVEY

Introduction

THE WHOLE RANGE OF EMOTIONS WE EXPERIENCE IN
EVERYDAY LIFE, BUT SUBLIMATED BY A WORD THAT
EVOKES THEM AND GATHERS THEM TOGETHER. THAT
WORD IS SPORT.

29 • Japan's Yukari Nakano swimming freestyle at the Japanese Open at Saitama
on April 20, 2008, to the music of *Capriccio Español*. Japan went on to win the team trials.

30-31 • The final barrier of the 110-meter hurdles at Rome's Golden Gala on June 3,
2007. American Anwar Moore, right, is slightly ahead and went on to beat
Cuba's Dayton Robles to the tape.

32-33 • Start of the Bart Cummings trophy at Melbourne's Flemington Racecourse,
on October 4, 2008. Viewed went on to win, ridden by Blake Shinn
(center, wearing the blue jersey).

34-35 • Scotland's Steve Frew, the reigning champion, competing in the rings discipline
during the 2006 Commonwealth Games in Melbourne.
Scotland finished fourth in the team event.

SHATTERED
DREAMS

- Misery for Australian rugby league player Jaiman Lowe after his team, the South Sydney Rabbitohs, was defeated 44-4 by the West Sydney Tigers, in the twelfth match of the National Rugby League season, on May 28, 2006.

INTRODUCTION Shattered Dreams

Probably no one is ever more disappointed and desperate than someone who achieves success only to see it snatched from his grasp, whether in sport or normal life. In a few cases however, the person who suffers the bitter disappointment of a lost victory has as a consequence become very famous.

Indeed, this happened in London in 1908, at the fourth Olympics, organized in great haste and hurry after Rome pulled out. The drama is captured in one of sport's most famous pictures: that of an athlete pushed to the very edge of endurance, being helped over the line by a judge and a doctor. The man was do-

• Tears from Japanese Asami Kitagawa after failing to win direct qualification to the final of the 200-meter medley at the Beijing Olympics on August 12, 2008.

INTRODUCTION Shattered Dreams

RANDO PIETRI AND HE WAS RUNNING THE MARATHON, THE GRU-
ELING RACE INVENTED BY DE COURBERTIN TO CELEBRATE THE
HEROIC GREEK MESSENGER WHO, IN REALITY NEVER EXISTED.
DORANDO PIETRO WAS BORN IN MANDRIO, A SMALL VILLAGE IN
CORREGGIO (REGGIO EMILIA), BUT HE LIVED WITH HIS FAMILY IN
CARPI, IN THE PROVINCE OF MODENA, WHERE HIS FATHER WAS
A GREENGROCER. HE WORKED AS A BICYCLE-RIDING DELIV-
ERYMAN FOR A BREAD SHOP. IN PARIS, PIETRI DISTINGUISHED
HIMSELF IN 1905 BY WINNING THE 30-KM (18.6 MILES) ROAD
RACE. THE FOLLOWING YEAR HE HAD TO PULL OUT OF THE
MARATHON AT THE ATHENS GAMES AND WAS NOT AMONG
THE FAVORITES WHEN HE ARRIVED FOR THE 1908 OLYMPICS.
DURING THE RACE HE CAME BACK FROM BEHIND, CATCHING
AND OVERHAULING THOSE WHO HAD TRIED TO BREAK OUT

TOO SOON. HOWEVER, WHEN HE ENTERED THE STADIUM, OUT IN FRONT AND ON HIS OWN, HE WAS IN A STATE OF EXTREME CONFUSION, FALLING OVER 5 TIMES IN THE SHORT 350-M (382 YARD) STRETCH BEFORE THE FINISHING LINE, WHICH HE TOOK 9 MINUTES TO COVER, HAVING TO BE REVIVED ON A NUMBER OF OCCASIONS BY MEDICAL STAFF. AFTER BEING ASSISTED TO THE LINE, HE RECOVERED WITH A GREAT DEAL OF HELP IN THE CHANGING ROOM (HE HAD TAKEN STRYCHNINE, THE DRUG OF CHOICE FOR RACERS BACK THEN, WHO TOOK HIGH DOSES), TO DISCOVER THAT HE HAD BEEN DISQUALIFIED FOR 'UNDUE ASSISTANCE,' THE OLYMPIC TITLE HAVING IN THE MEANTIME BEEN AWARDED TO THE SECOND PLACED AMERICAN, HAYES. ON THE INITIATIVE OF THE WRITER ARTHUR CONAN DOYLE, THE CREATOR OF SHERLOCK HOLMES, QUEEN ALEXANDRA PRE-

Shattered Dreams

Introduction

SENTED HIM WITH A SPECIAL TROPHY THE NEXT DAY, IN PARTIAL CONSOLATION FOR THAT LOST VICTORY.

OUR FASCINATION WITH THE MARATHON BEGAN THEN AND WAS FURTHER STIMULATED BY A SERIES OF REVENGE WINS FOR PIETRI, ABOVE ALL IN THE UNITED STATES, WHERE HE HAD NOW BECOME A PROFESSIONAL. HE EARNED A LOT OF MONEY BUT LOST IT ALL IN BAD INVESTMENTS, ENDING UP AS A DRIVER IN SAN REMO, WHERE HE DIED IN 1942. "I STAND IN SOLIDARITY WITH ALL THOSE WHO HAVE WON AND LOST THEIR VICTORY," HE WROTE OF HIMSELF. HIS NAME, DORANDO, WILL FOREVER STAND FOR THE MOST EXCRUCIATING AND BITTER DISAPPOINTMENT IN THE HISTORY OF SPORT.

Roma's Francesco Totti pleads to the heavens for help during a match against Inter Milan at the San Siro on February 27, 2008.

44 ● Dustin Pedroia of the Boston Red Sox is angry after being hit by a pitch from Tampa Bay's Matt Garza in game seven of the 2008 American League playoffs, in St Petersburg, Florida.

45 ● Pedroia despairs during game seven of the playoffs against Tampa Bay, which Boston lost 3-1.

46 • Jonathan Thurston of the Queensland Cowboys leaves the pitch disappointed on August 16, 2008 in Townsville, after his team lost to the Gold Coast Titans four matches from the end of the season.

47 • Manny Ramirez of the Los Angeles Dodgers is disconsolate after getting out in the seventh innings of a Major League baseball game against Philadelphia Phillies on August 13, 2008.

Munich, September 1, 2007: the disappointment of Germany's Marcel Hacker, foreground, is obvious at the World Rowing Championships, beaten by a whisker to the singles title by New Zealand's Mahe Drysdale.

American boxer Jameel McCline is consoled by his Russian opponent, Nikolay Valuyev, who beat him for the WBA world heavyweight title in Basel, Switzerland on January 20, 2007.

52 ● Rahul Dravid, former captain of the Indian cricket team, has his head down after being dismissed by Australia's Shane Watson during the Nagpur test match on November 9, 2008. India won by 172 runs.

53 ● Shattered, German Michael Greis reflects on the bad day that saw him finish 15th in the pursuit at the 'bike and shoot' World Cup biathlon at Erfurt on January 7, 2007.

Switzerland's Sibylle Matter despairs after being forced to withdraw in the cycle leg of the World Triathlon Championships in 2003, held in Queenstown, New Zealand. The Swiss champion that year, Matter is also a renowned sports doctor.

56-57 ● American Shalane Flanagan breaks down after crossing the line in third place in the 10,000 meters at the 2008 Beijing Games, behind two Ethiopians. Flanagan beat the US record by 12 seconds, two days after suffering food poisoning.

57 ● Facing her sister Venus in the Wimbledon final on July 5, 2008, Serena Williams seems to be contemplating the strategy she should adopt. Venus ended up winning 7-5, 6-4.

58-59 ● US tennis player James Blake can't hide his disappointment over an error committed in a match against Croat Ivo Karlovic in the third round of the PTA indoor tournament on October 25, 2007 in Basel.

59 ● A very disappointed Rafael Nadal during a change of ends in his match against Argentinean David Nalbandian in the final of the PTA Masters at Paris Bercy on November 4, 2007. Nalbandian won in straight sets, 6-4, 6-0.

● Hungarian Agnes Szávay looks like she wants to hide her face after an error against China's Jie Zheng in the fourth round match at Wimbledon 2008, which Zheng won 6-3, 6-4.

62-63 • Russian Marat Safin is angry with himself over a mishit in his first-round match in the 2009 Australian Open in Melbourne against Spanish Ivan Navarro. Safin eventually won in three sets, 6-3, 6-3, 6-4.

63 • Navarro curses himself for an error in the match against Safin in the first round of the 2009 Australian Open at Melbourne Park on January 19.

64-65 • Russian-born Canadian Olga Ovtchinnikova sinks in desperation after her defeat to Poland's Aleksandra Socha in the Canada-Poland team fencing match at the 2008 Beijing Olympics.

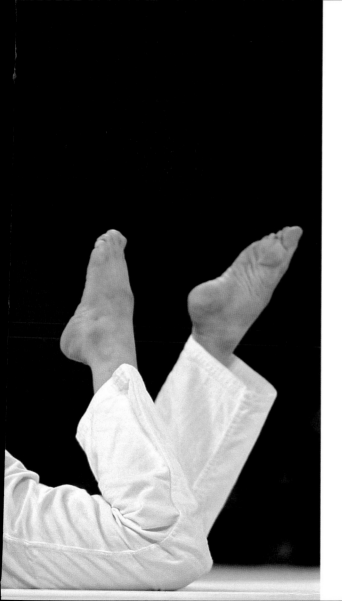

• Algerian Lila Latrous, of Estonian origin, cries with rage after her defeat to China's Xu Yan in her preliminary judo bout at the 2008 Beijing Olympic Games. Xu won the bronze medal in the 57 kg category, while the gold went to Italy's Giulia Quintavalle.

68 ● A reaction of despair from Japanese judoka Hiroaki Hiraoka after her defeat to American Taraje Williams-Murray in the 60 kg preliminary judo bout at the 2008 Olympics.

69 ● Russian judoka Alim Gadanov is inconsolable after his semi-final defeat in the 66 kg class at the 2008 Beijing Games by France's Benjamin Darbelet, who won the silver, relegating Gardanov to fifth place.

70 • Puerto Rican Carlos Delgado of the New York Mets throws his bat away in disappointment after being struck out by a Boston Red Sox pitcher in a practice match at Port Sainte Lucie in Florida on March 15, 2007. The Mets went on to win 4-1.

71 • England's Andrew Flintoff leaves the ground after having been bowled by India's Ishant Sharma during the fourth one-day international match between India and England in Bangalore on November 23, 2008.

• Kamghe Gaba (with a Chadian father and German mother, representing Germany) grimaces as he gets up and carries on after colliding with Polish Daniel Dabrowski in the final of the 4x400 meter relay at the World Championships in Osaka in 2007.

74 ● Denmark goes down to Croatia in the quarterfinals of the Olympic handball tournament at the Beijing Games. Central defender Jesper Jensen cannot hide his disappointment.

75 ● "Did I really do it?" asks Britain's Andy Turner after a heat of the 110-meter hurdles at the 2008 Beijing Games. Having come last in the heats four years earlier, Turner, who appears disappointed, managed to qualify for the second round, where he was one of the first to be eliminated.

76 • A zero on his third throw drove German Ralf Bartels to despair in the final of the shot put at the World Athletics Championships at Osaka in 2007. The German qualified in fifth position but finished seventh overall.

77 • A playoff for bronze at the 2008 Beijing Games between Croatia and Spain: Croatian left winger Goran Sprem could not hide his disappointment at the 35-29 defeat, a clear step backwards after the gold his country won in Athens in 2004.

78 • Floods of tears for American Nicole Teter in the 800-meter heats at the 2008 Beijing Olympic Games. Teter had to withdraw after the recurrence of a pulled muscle.

78-79 • Mechelle Lewis tries in vain to comfort the USA's Torri Edwards, who has just failed to hand over the baton to team-mate Lauryn Williams in the 4x100 meter heat at the 2008 Beijing Games.

80 • A picture of disappointment: German Tina Bachmann, right back, can't come to terms with their 3-1 defeat to Argentina's 3-1 for the hockey bronze medal at the 2008 Beijing Games.

81 • Lashinda Demus drops to the ground, unable to get up, having failed to qualify for the 2008 Olympics during the final of the 100-meter hurdles at the US Track and Field Trials in Eugene, Oregon, on June 29, 2008.

82 ● Having missed an easy goal, attacker Andrew Lovett of the Essendon Bombers despairs during the local Melbourne derby match against the Carlton Blues, played on May 14, 2006 during the Australian Rules football national championship.

83 ● Swansea City's French goalkeeper, Willy Guéret, is disconsolate after his team's defeat on penalties in the final of the English League One playoffs (equivalent to Italy's Serie C) against Barnsley in Cardiff on May 27, 2006.

84 ● English rugby player Hugo Ellis reacts after England's 20-6 defeat to Ireland in an Under-20s match in Athlone on February 23, 2007.

85 ● French Remi Martin appears distraught at the end of the elimination-round match in rugby's European Cup. His team, Stade Français, collapsed away from home to Bristol by 17-0 on November 18, 2007. Neither side made it to the quarterfinals.

86 • Cleveland Browns receiver Braylon Edwards cannot believe his side's 28-9 defeat away to the Tennessee Titans in Nashville on December 7, 2008. The Titans' victory won them the American Football Conference South title.

87 • Kansas Chiefs attacker Branden Albert broken-heartedly removes his mask after the end of a National Football League match in September of 2008 in Atlanta, in which the Chiefs succumbed by 38-14 to the Atlanta Falcons.

Britain's Nick Dempsy is dog tired and disappointed with his windsurfing performance in the first trial of the sailboard race for the 2008 Beijing Games. He recovered to fight for a medal, finishing in fourth, just six points away from the bronze.

A perfectionist: Daniel Smith, the Australian swimmer, is just 14 years old. He is seen here winning one of his eight gold medals at the Sydney youth championships in January 2007. Despite his victory, he still managed to appear disappointed about his time.

92 • A curious expression for South African swimmer Natalie du Toit in a heat of the 100-meter freestyle at the Beijing Paralympics.

93 • Japan's Hane Ito seems dissatisfied at the end of the 100-meter backstroke heat at the 2008 Beijing Games, despite qualifying easily for the next round.

94-95 • Chilean Arturo Vidal of Bayer Leverkusen despairs after his team's 2-1 defeat in Munich on March 22, 2008. Bayern Munich's win brought them to within one point of their 21st German football league (Bundesliga) title. Bayer finished seventh.

95 • Dejected Hamburg footballer Benjamin Lauth lies on the ground after his team's 0-1 defeat away at the hands of Wolfsburg in the Bundesliga 2006-2007, on November 4, 2006.

Croatian defender Vedran Corluka looks disconsolate, but is actually thanking the heavens for having scored the decisive penalty that gave his team, Manchester City, a place in the third round of the UEFA Cup, beating the Danish team, Midtjylland, on August 28, 2008 in Herning.

98-99 ● The goalkeeper for the Italian Under-21 team, Gianluca Curci from Roma, despairs in Portugal's Aveiro Stadium, after Holland achieved a 2-2 draw to go through to the semifinals. Holland went on to win the title, beating Ukraine 3-0.

100-101 ● Peruvian attacker Claudio Pizarro cannot hide his disappointment after his Werder Bremen team lost 3-1 to Bayern Munich in October of 2006.

102 • Disappointment for Alemannia Aachen goalkeeper, Thorsten Stuckmann, after the end of an away game to Hamburg at St. Pauli on October 5, 2008, which the home team won.

102-103 • Luca Toni is angry after missing a shot for Bayern away to Hamburg on January 30, 2009. Hamburg won 1-0.

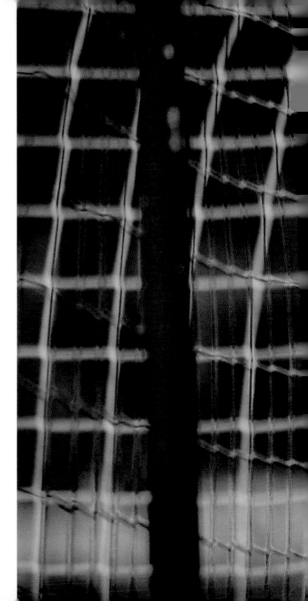

MOMENTS
of GLORY

- Terence Williams of the Louisville Cardinals is happy after a successful defensive play against Marshall University in September of 2007.

INTRODUCTION Moments of Glory

SUCCESS AT SPORT BRINGS VARYING BUT CONSISTENTLY GREAT JOY, ENTHUSIASM, AND SATISFACTION. ALTHOUGH IT IS DIFFICULT TO MEASURE IN ABSOLUTE TERMS, THE CASE WE RECOUNT BELOW MAY WELL REPRESENT THE VERY PINNACLE OF SATISFACTION THAT SUCCESS CAN BRING, ESPECIALLY IF WE TAKE INTO ACCOUNT THE CONDITIONS UNDER WHICH IT WAS GAINED.

IT TOOK PLACE IN 1904 IN ST LOUIS, THE THEN CAPITAL OF LOUISIANA AND NOW OF MISSOURI, WHERE THE THIRD EVER OLYMPIC GAMES WERE HELD IN CONDITIONS OF INDESCRIBABLE CONFUSION. THERE WERE CIRCUS SHOWS AND COMPETITIONS THAT CLEARLY

- A joyful hug between AC Milan players Seedorf and Kakà during the Livorno-Milan match of April 27, 2008, after Seedorf had scored the Rossoneri's fourth goal in a 4-1 victory.

INTRODUCTION Moments of Glory

FELL BELOW OLYMPIC STANDARD AND THE GAMES OC-CURRED IN THE CONTEXT OF THE LOUISIANA WORLD TRADE FAIR. VERY FEW NORTH AMERICANS HAD YET TAKEN PART IN THE OLYMPIC ADVENTURE, WHICH WAS YET TO BECOME THE FOCAL POINT OF AN ATHLETE'S CAREER. IT HAD JUST BEEN EIGHT YEARS SINCE DE COUBERTIN HAD REVIVED THE GAMES. THE BARON HIM-SELF WAS NOT THERE AND THERE WERE JUST OVER 600 HUNDRED ATHLETES REPRESENTING A DOZEN COUN-TRIES AND WITH NO ITALIAN PARTICIPATION.

GYMNASTICS WERE VERY POPULAR AND WERE DIVIDED INTO 'SWEDISH' AND 'GERMAN': THE FORMER WERE MAINLY EXERCISES ON EQUIPMENT, WHILE THE LATTER ALSO INCLUDED COMPETITIONS THAT WERE SUBSE-

INTRODUCTION Moments of Glory

QUENTLY ABSORBED INTO ATHLETICS, SUCH AS RUN-
NING, JUMPING AND THROWING. MANY EUROPEAN EMI-
GRANTS TOOK PART IN BOTH (GERMANS, AUSTRIAN,
AND SWISS) WHO TRADITIONALLY PRACTICED GYMNAS-
TICS. ONE OF THESE WAS GEORG EYSER, NO LONGER
VERY YOUNG, HAVING BEEN BORN IN KIEL IN GERMANY
IN 1871, AND THEN MOVING WITH HIS FAMILY TO ST
LOUIS, WHERE HE BECAME AN AMERICAN CITIZEN AND
MEMBER OF THE LOCAL CLUB, THE CONCORDIA. EYSER
LEFT THOSE GAMES WITH 6 MEDALS, INCLUDING 3
GOLDS: THE PARALLEL BARS, ROPE CLIMBING AND
EQUESTRIAN TEAM EVENTING, ALTHOUGH HE FINISHED
71ST AND LAST IN THE TEAM EVENTING. HE CAME LAST
IN THE SPEED AND DISTANCE TRIALS FOR A VERY GOOD

Moments of Glory

REASON. HE HAD A WOODEN LEG. HE HAD BEEN RUN OVER BY A TRAIN AS A BOY AND BY FORCE OF WILL HAD TURNED HIMSELF INTO AN EXCELLENT GYMNAST, DESPITE HIS HANDICAP. EVEN THOUGH WE DO NOT EVEN HAVE A PICTURE OF HIM WE KNOW THAT HE WAS SO HUGELY PLEASED WITH HIS SIX PODIUM PLACES THAT HE TOOK HIS CLUB ABROAD FOR A COMPETITION IN FRANKFURT. THE FOLLOWING YEAR HE WON THE INTERNATIONAL TOURNAMENT AT CINCINNATI. HE SUBSEQUENTLY DISAPPEARED BUT HIS INCREDIBLE JOY IS STILL ECHOING DOWN TO US MORE THAN A CENTURY AFTER THE EVENT.

- You can still hear Vale's shout of delight: Valentina Vezzali winning in the final of the individual saber at the 2008 Beijing Olympics, beating South Korea's Nam Hyunhee. It was the fifth Olympic gold of Vezzali's career.

112 • Joy for Dallas Cowboys defender DeMarcus Ware after successfully body-checking the Washington Redskins quarterback during an American Football game on December 30, 2007 in Landover.

113 • The Cincinnati Bengals receiver is held aloft by a team-mate to celebrate the team's first touchdown in an away game against the Miami Dolphins on December 30, 2007.

114 • Brazil's Diego celebrates his first goal against Belgium in the third-place match at the 2008 Beijing Games.

115 • Defender Frostee Rucker (92) of the Cincinnati Bengals rejoices at the touchdown scored by his team-mate Chinedum Ndukwe (41) in an NFL match against the Miami Dolphins on December 30, 2007 in Florida, which the Bengals went on to win 38-25.

Celebrations in advance: Patrick Cobbs of the Miami Dolphins rejoices as he is left on his own to score in an NFL pre-season game away to the Kansas City Chiefs in August of 2007.

118 ● Materazzi looks like he wants to bite Ibrahimovic's head off. In fact he is expressing his joy at Ibra's penalty goal in the 13th minute of the first half, which broke the deadlock for Inter Milan against Reggina at the San Siro on March 8, 2008.

119 ● Tennessee Volunteers players pile on top of each other to celebrate the touchdown by Nevein McKenzie (left) that gave his team a 14-7 lead over the UCLA Bruins in Pasadena on September 1, 2008.

120-121 • Cassio jumps into the arms of Angelo Costanzo after the final whistle gave victory to Adelaide United against the Kashima Antlers in the Australian Rules football quarterfinal playoffs.

121 • Manu Vatuvei of the New Zealand Warriors celebrates after scoring a try against the Penrith Panthers in the 25th match of the 2008 Australian Rugby League championship in Auckland.

Spain go down 118-107: basketball's Dream Team USA explode with delight at the 2008 Olympic Games, after winning the gold medal in the final on 24 August, the final day of the Games.

124 • Three Chicago Bears players jump for joy (from left, Kevin Payne, Brandon McGowan and Nathan Vasher) at a successful defensive play during an NFL match on December 7, 2008 away to the Indianapolis Colts.

125 • Inter Milan's Zlatan Ibrahimovic jumps on Maicon after his 33rd-minute goal against Sampdoria at Marassi on August 30, 2008. Delvecchio went on to equalize for Sampdoria in the 68th minute.

126 • Juventus' David Trézéguet is literally lifted up by his team-mate Vincenzo Iaquinta. They were the goal-scorers in the 5-1 thrashing of Livorno in the opening match of the 2007-08 season. The Frenchman scored a hat trick and Iaquinta bagged two (including a penalty).

127 • Inter Milan's Victor Obinna, with his tongue out, jumps on Ibrahimovic's back to celebrate the Swede's goal at the Stadio Olimpico. Inter won 4-0 with a brace from Ibra, Stankovic put away the third and Obinna scored the fourth.

128 • Jonathan Broxton (left) and Manny Ramirez exchange high-fives after the Los Angeles Dodgers beat the San Diego Padres 6-3 on September 3, 2008 in Los Angeles.

129 • Right, Matt Kemp (27) and Andre Ethier of the Dodgers celebrate the win over the Padres mentioned in the photo above.

130 • China's Shen Qijong rejoices after a 3-2 win over Japan in the qualifying round of the volleyball at the 2008 Beijing Olympics. China went through to the quarterfinals while Japan finished last.

131 • Spaniard Pau Gasol lets out a victory cry after Spain's 91-86 win over Lithuania in the basketball semifinals at the 2008 Beijing Games.

132 • American Lindsey Vonn shows her delight at winning in the Super Gs at the World Cup of Skiing in Val d'Isère on February 3, 2009.

133 • Germany's Maria Riesch, left, and American Julia Mancuso are both happy after Riesch won the combined event in the World Cup of Skiing at St Anton, Austria in December of 2007.

134 ● Manchester United forward Wayne Rooney celebrates his first goal at home in the Premier League game against West Bromwich Albion on October 18, 2008.

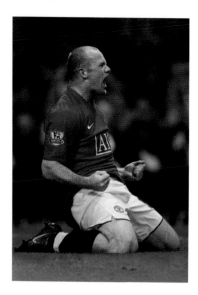

135 ● May 12, 2007: his team have just made it 2-2 away to Bochum and Stuttgart goalkeeper Timo Hildebrand can't hide his delight. Stuttgart went on to win the game 3-2 and clinch the league title.

136-137 • Everyone dives in to congratulate Nihat Kahveci, buried under his team-mates after scoring the decisive goal in Turkey's win against the Czech Republic in football's European Championships in Geneva in June of 2008.

137 • A joyful somersault by Liverpool's Robbie Keane in celebration of his Champions League goal at home against Eindhoven on October 1, 2008.

KAUZER

Slovenia's Peter Kauzer celebrates at the end of the K1 kayaking slalom semifinal at the 2008 Beijing Games. Despite having the best time, Kauzer didn't make the final due to the penalty points he had accrued.

140 • South Africa's Kevin Paul celebrates his success in the 100-meter breaststroke at the Beijing Paralympics on September 10, 2008.

141 • The joy of American Michael Phelps is easy to understand, as this win in the 100-meter butterfly at the 2008 Beijing Games equaled Mark Spitz's record of seven golds in one Olympics, which he then went on to better with his victory in the 4x100-meter medley.

142 • Short-lived joy for American Hayley McGregory, who has just beaten the 100-meter backstroke world record at the 2008 US Olympic swimming trials in Omaha. The record was beaten in the next heat.

142-143 • Timeless joy: Dara Torres thanks the heavens for her silver in the 50-meter freestyle at the 2008 Beijing Games. The 41-year-old swimmer, back at the Olympics after 16 years, won three silver medals.

144-145 ● Brothers Mario (left) and Xavier García celebrate the bronze won by Spain in the World Water Polo Championships held in Melbourne, thanks to a victory over Serbia.

145 ● Croatia's Samir Barac celebrates after the victory over Hungary that gave his team the world water polo title in Melbourne on April 1, 2007.

The fifth stage of the 2008 Tour de France, from Cholet to Chateauroux, on July 9. Britain's Mark Cavendish dominated the sprint and celebrates by punching the air.

● Jamaican Shelly-Ann Fraser celebrates her success in the final of the 100 meters at the 2008 Beijing Olympics, won in 10.78 seconds, two meters ahead of her two compatriots, Sherone Simpson and Kerron Stewart.

150-151 • A joyous lap of honor with her country's flag for Jamaica's Melanie Walker, who has just won the 400-meter hurdles at the 2008 Beijing Games.

151 • Draped in the American flag, Bryan Clay shows his feelings at having won the gold in the decathlon at the 2008 Beijing Games.

Argentina's Maria Magdalena Alcega is lifted up by her team-mates to celebrate the 3-1 win over Germany that gave the South Americans the bronze medal in field hockey at the 2008 Beijing Olympics.

Carried aloft in triumph by fans, Australian Anthony Mundine celebrates his success in boxing's WBA super-middleweight world title fight against compatriot Danny Green on May 17, 2006 in Sydney.

It's joy rather than desperation that the Czech Republic's David Kostelecky is expressing after winning the men's trap at the 2008 Beijing Games.

Iranian Hadi Sael blows kisses of delight after beating Italian Mauro Sarmiento in the 80 kg taekwondo final at the 2008 Beijing Olympics.

160 • Mexico's Guillermo Pérez has just won the 58 kg gold at the 2008 Olympics against the Dominican Republic's Yulis Mercedes.

160-161 • A short burst of joy for Italian Mauro Sarmento, who qualified for the final of the 80 kg taekwondo at the Beijing Games. Sarmento beat Britain's Aaron Cook, but then went on to lose later in the competition.

162 • American Alexander Artem having successfully completed his routine on the pommel horse at the USA 2008 Olympic Trials in Philadelphia.

163 • Satisfaction mixed with tears: this was the reaction of Norwegian Olaf Tufte after winning gold in the final of the single sculls at the 2008 Beijing Olympics.

164 ● German Matthias Steiner celebrates the lift that guaranteed him gold in the 105 kg class at the 2008 Beijing Games.

165 ● More joy for Steiner. Born in Vienna, he became a German citizen and had finished seventh for Austria at the 2004 Olympics.

Indonesia's Sandow Weldemar Nasution kisses the bar after a lift at the 2008 Beijing Games. He went on to finish 11th with a total of 347 kg in the 77 kg category.

168-169 ● Spain's Rafael Nadal, the eventual winner, does a somersault in delight after match point against Switzerland's Roger Federer in the final of the Rome Masters tennis competition on May 14, 2006.

169 ● More Nadal joy; this time after a successful shot against Federer, again in the 2006 Rome Masters.

170 • Satisfaction for Russian Anna Chicherova after a successful jump in the high jump final at the 2008 Beijing Games, in which she won the bronze medal.

171 • Brazil's Fabiana de Oliveira buries her face in her hands while celebrating a win over the USA that gave the South Americans their water polo gold medal at the 2008 Olympics.

Russia's Yelena Isinbayeva shows her delight at her new pole vaulting world record of 5.05 meters, which crowned her success at the 2008 Beijing Games.

174 ● Russian Maxim Chudov rejoices after the 4x7.5 km relay victory in the World Biathlon Championship on February 16, 2008 at Ostersund in Sweden.

174-175 ● Norway's Ola Vigen Hattestad is exultant after victory in the sprint at the World Cross-country Skiing Cup on December 14, 2008 at Davos, Switzerland.

176 • Australian jockey Craig Newitt greets his success in the sixth race at Caulfield in Melbourne on August 16, 2008, with a pat for his horse, Light Fantastic.

177 • French jockey Olivier Doleuze kisses his horse, Good Ba Ba, after winning the Champions Mile at the Hong Kong race track on April 27, 2008.

178-179 ● Derek Jeter pats the helmet of his team-mate Bobby Abreu after a run scored by the New York Yankees away to the Los Angeles Angels in Anaheim on September 9, 2008.

179 ● Eric Barton (50) and Darrelle Revis celebrate a 20-14 win for the New York Jets away to the Miami Dolphins in the 2008-09 NFL season.

180 • Applause and tears from Norway's Kjersti Tysse Platzer after winning the silver medal in the 20 km walk at the 2008 Beijing Games.

181 • Italy's Elisa Rigaudo smiles, having won the bronze medal in the 20 km walk at the Beijing Olympcis, just five seconds behind Platzer (above photo).

182 • Vasyl Lomanchenko hides tears of joy in the Ukrainian flag after beating France's Khedafi Djelkir in the 57 kg boxing final at the 2008 Beijing Games.

182-183 • A flag on his shoulder and a broad smile for Sudan's Ismael Ahmed Ismail, whose second-place finish in the 800 meters at the 2008 Beijing Games gave his country its first ever Olympic medal.

184-185 • UCLA Bruins team-mates surround Ryan Moya (15) after his touchdown in the last minute of the NFL game against the Tennessee Volunteers on September 1, 2008 at Pasadena.

185 • Deportivo La Coruña players hug each other after their second goal against Real Madrid at home in the Spanish Football League on August 31, 2008.

186 • Jon Beason (52) and Charles Johnson (95) of the Carolina Panthers celebrate a successful defensive action in a 2008 NFL game against the San Diego Chargers.

187 • Jacksonville Jaguars receiver Reggie Williams (11) hugs his team-mate Quin Gray (5) after a touchdown against the Oakland Raiders, en route to a 49-11 win that propelled them into the NFL playoffs.

188 • Celebrations for South Korea's handball bronze medal at the 2008 Beijing Olympics, with a win over Hungary.

189 • Brazilians Steinbrecher, Castro, de Olivera and Claudino hug after beating the USA to win gold in the volleyball final at the 2008 Beijing Games.

190-191 • Valentina Vezzali is hugged by team-mates Salvatori, Trillini and Granbassi after Italy's win in the match for the foil team bronze against Hungary at the 2008 Beijing Games.

191 • Italy's Aldo Montano dances with joy after winning against Russia's Stanislav Pozdnyakov in the match that won Italy the saber team bronze medal at the 2008 Olympics.

192 • Reed Doughty (37) of the Washington Redskins celebrates his interception of a pass in the end zone by the Dallas Cowboys. The Redskins won 27-6 at Landover on December 30, 2007.

193 • Twickenham, September 6, 2008: Ugo Monye (left) of Harlequins receives the congratulations of team-mate Davis Trettle after scoring a try against Saracens in the English rugby championship.

194 • Tiger Woods is exultant after scoring a birdie on the 18th hole that guaranteed a play-off against Rocco Mediate at the 108th US Open at San Diego on June 15, 2008.

195 • Luca Toni rejoices after the first goal against Aris Salonicc, which opened the floodgates for Bayern Munich at home. Bayern went on to beat the Greeks 6-0 in the Champions League game on December 19, 2007.

196 • Andrés Marcelo Nocioni throws a friendly celebratory punch at team-mate
Leonardo Martin Gutierrez (12) to celebrate the basketball bronze medal won by Brazil
against Lithuania at the 2008 Olympics.

197 • Brett Deledio, hugged by team-mate Mark Coughlan (24), celebrates a goal by the
Richmond Tigers against the Adelaide Crows in an Australian Football League match in
Melbourne on May 20, 2006.

198 ● Miami Dolphins defender Jason Taylor celebrates a successful defensive play against the Baltimore Ravens in a 2007 NFL game in Miami, won 22-16 by the Dolphins.

199 ● Joey Porter of the Miami Dolphins shouts for joy at the crowd during an NFL game against the Buffalo Bills on October 26, 2008, which Miami won by 25-16.

● The Philadelphia Phillies' Carlos Ruiz dashes towards Brad Lidge, who has just rounded the bases, after a strike-out against Eric Hinske of the Tampa Bay Rays. The Phillies won this game, the 5th of the 2008 World Series, by 4-3.

202 • Italian walker Alex Schwazer thanks the heavens at the 2008 Beijing Games after winning the gold medal in the 50 km.

203 • Joy and tears on the face of Schwarzer for his success in the 50 km walk at the 2008 Olympics, which he won by two and a half minutes over the Australian Tallent.

A shout that shook the world: Jamaica's Usain Bolt has just won the 200 meter final at the 2008 Beijing Games, in a time of 19.3 seconds. That time set a new world record and was the second of Bolt's three golds and three world records in this Olympics.

206-207 • German Stefan Bradl lets go of the handlebars of his Aprilia and raises his fists to celebrate his second-place finish in the 125s at the World Motorcycle Championship in Sachsenring in July of 2008. He went on to win two tests and finish third in the final table.

207 • Spain's Alvaro Bautista jumps into the arms of his manager, Jorge Aspar of Master-MVA, after his second-place finish in the 250cc race at Jerez in the 2007 World Motorcycle Championship.

208 • Valentino Rossi does a wheelie on his Yamaha after achieving second place in the starting grid for the MotoGP race at Donington on June 23, 2007. Rossi went on to finish fourth.

209 • Valentino celebrating again after winning the Estoril Grand Prix at the 2007 MotoGP.

210-211 • Champagne and smiles
for Nelsinho Piquet (Renault, center)
and McLaren's Lewis Hamilton,
who were second and first at
Hockenheim, respectively,
in the Formula 1 Grand Prix in 2008.

211 • Joy and champagne for Lewis
Hamilton, winner at Silverstone in Formula
1 in 2008 with his McLaren-Mercedes.

212 • Another triumph for Lewis Hamilton and McLaren, this time at Monte Carlo in the 2008 Formula 1 Grand Prix.

212-213 • Britain's Lewis Hamilton, just after emerging from his McLaren-Mercedes to celebrate his success at the Formula 1 Grand Prix at Hockenheim.

214 • Jimmie Johnson celebrates his win with Chevrolet at the NASCAR 500 on August 31, 2008 in Fontana, California.

214-215 • Jimmie Johnson again cheered by the crowd after his win in Fontana, in the season when he won the final of the NASCAR Sprint Cup for the third consecutive time.

216 ● Spain's Rafael Nadal is weary but delighted as he lies on the ground after winning match point against compatriot Fernando Verdasco in the semifinal of the 2009 Australian Open.

217 ● Ana Ivanovic celebrates a point won against France's Alize Cornet in the second round of the Chinese Tennis Open. China's Jieng Zhe knocked out Ivanovic in the quarterfinals.

218 ● US twins Mike and Bob Bryan embrace after winning the doubles title at the 2008 US Open at Flushing Meadows.

218-219 ● American Liezel Huber and Cara Black of Zimbabwe about to fly into each others' arms, having beaten Raymond (USA) and Stosur (Australia) for the doubles title at the 2008 US Open.

220-221 • China's Zhang Xiaoping is applauded by the public after knocking his Algerian rival, Abdelhafid Benchabla, to the canvas in the quarterfinals of the 81 kg boxing tournament at the 2008 Beijing Games. Zhang won on points.

221 • Zhang again, celebrating after his win over Benchabla. Zhang went on to win the gold medal, beating Ireland's Kenny Egan in the final.

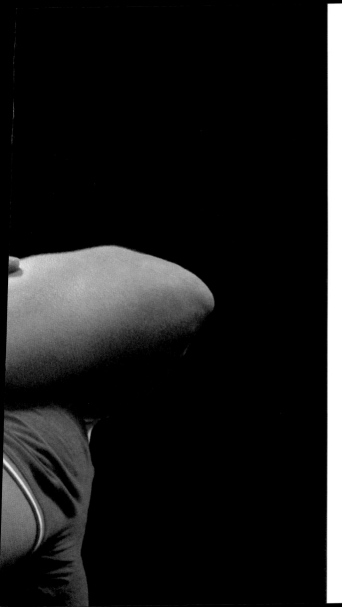

● Italian Super Heavyweight boxer, Roberto Cammarelle, hugged by coach Francesco Damiani after his victory in the final at the 2008 Beijing Games against China's Zhang Zhilei.

224 ● Britain's James DeGale on his knees, celebrating his win over Cuban Emilio Correa Bayeaux in the 75 kg Olympic boxing final at the 2008 Beijing Games.

224-225 ● Ukraine's Vasyl Lomachenko, red vest, jumps for joy after beating France's Khedafi Djelkir in the 57 kg boxing final at the 2008 Beijing Games.

France's Julien Pillet cannot hide his delight after France's victory over the USA in the saber team final at the 2008 Beijing Games.

● China's Lin Dan, having just beaten Malaysia's Lee Chong Wei in the badminton singles final at the 2008 Beijing Games. Four years before, in Athens, Lin Dan was knocked out in the first round, Lee in the second.

Serena Williams shouts for joy after beating Serbia's Jelena Jankovic in the final of the 2008 US Open, for her ninth Grand Slam victory.

232 ● Ukraine's Bill Priddy celebrates the USA's victory against Brazil in the volleyball final at the 2008 Beijing Olympics.

233 ● American tennis player Serena Williams shows her joy at winning match point in the quarterfinals of the 2009 Australian Open against Denmark's Caroline Wozniacki.

- Tiger Woods is delighted about his birdie on the 18th hole, which took him into a play-off with Rocco Mediate in the 2008 US Open at San Diego. Woods eventually won, on his 91st hole for the tournament.

Poland's Kacper Kozlowski shouts in jubilation as he breaks the tape at the end of the 4x400 meters, helping Poland win the bronze ahead of Jamaica at the 2007 World Athletics Championship in Osaka.

238 • Amit Mishra is held aloft by team-
mate Harbhajan Singh after catching an
Australian batsman in the third test match
between India and Australia in Delhi, on
November 1, 2008.

238-239 • Another batsman out: this
time Indian Virender Sehwag is hugged by
Anil Kumble during the same India-
Australia test match.

• These two pictures show the passionate enthusiasm of Valentina Vezzali at the 2008 Beijing Games, after winning the fifth gold medal of her career, in the individual saber competition.

242 • Steve Smith of the Carolina Panthers celebrates a successful catch during an NFL 2008-09 pre-season match against the Washington Redskins at Charlotte on August 23, 2008.

243 • Donovan McNabb (5) congratulates his Philadelphia Eagles team-mate Brian Westbrook after a touchdown against the St Louis Rams in an NFL home game in September 2008.

244 • Spain's Dani Pedrosa congratulates himself after winning the fourth stage of the Shanghai MotoGP on May 14, 2008.

245 • Sitting astride his Honda, Britain's James Toseland acknowledges his win in the first race of the 2007 World Superbike Championship, at Donington on April 1.

246 • "I've won!" is what Britain's Lewis Hamilton seems to be saying by holding up his fingers after his victory in the Formula 1 Grand Prix in Montecarlo on May 25, 2008.

247 • Hamilton again, in the cockpit of his McLaren-Mercedes, celebrates his win in the Belgian Formula 1 Grand Prix on September 7, 2008.

248 • Nashville, Tennessee, March 3, 2009: Jason Arnott of the Nashville Predators is delighted with his extra-time goal in the NHL game against the Edmonton Oilers.

249 • Rick Nash of the Columbus Blue Jackets just after scoring the second of three goals against the Edmonton Oilers on December 31, 2007 in the NHL. His first was a long distance shot, followed by a short tap-in, and his third was an empty net goal.

250 • Albert Pujols of the St Louis Cardinals (left) celebrates together with team-mate Yadier Molina after taking the lead (4-3) over the Houston Astros at home on May 31, 2006.

251 • "I'm the best!" shouts Francisco Rodriguez of the Los Angeles Angels after leading his team to a 7-4 victory over the Seattle Mariners in Anaheim in 2008, and achieving a record of 57 saves in the process.

252 • Oklahoma State receivers, Dez Bryant (1) and Adarius Bowman have a mid-air hug to celebrate a touchdown scored against Indiana University in the Insight Bowl at Tempe, Arizona, on December 31, 2007.

253 • Akinori Iwamura (1) is lifted up by Cliff Floyd after the Tampa Bay Devil Rays win over the Boston Red Sox in the 7th match of the American League baseball season on October 19, 2008 in St Petersburg, Florida.

● The irrepressible
enthusiasm of Brazil's
Fernanda Oliveira
(standing) and Isabel
Swan at their third
place in sailing's dinghy
class at the 2008
Beijing Games.

256 • Kyle Bush, having just climbed out of his Toyota to cavort with the checkered flag after his win in the Las Vegas test of the 2009 NASCAR Sprint Cup.

256-257 • Kyle Bush dances on his Toyota after his win in Las Vegas on March 1, 2009, which he followed with another two victories that month.

● The US four-man bobsleigh team, piloted by Steven Holcomb, is congratulated by fans after their win at the 2009 World Championships at Lake Placid.

FAST
to the
FINISH

Valentino Rossi on his Yamaha in the qualifiers for the MotoGP at Estoril on April 12, 2008.

INTRODUCTION Fast to the Finish

USUALLY WE ASSOCIATE SPEED IN SPORT WITH SPRINTING, THE FASTEST POSSIBLE AVERAGE TIME, THE WINNING BURST IN A CYCLE RACE, AND THE WINNERS OF CAR OR MOTORBIKE RACES. CERTAINLY SPEED IS REALLY FASCINATING: THE FASTEST MAN OR WOMAN IN THE WORLD IS ALWAYS ONE OF THE MOST GLAMOROUS AND TALKED ABOUT PEOPLE IN SPORT. HOWEVER, SPEED IS MORE THAN THIS. WHEN WE TALK ABOUT A FOOTBALL WIZARD, PRAISING THE SPEED OF HIS DRIBBLING, OF A MOVE, OF A SWERVE TOWARD GOAL WE ARE EXTOLLING AN OVERALL ABILITY, THE FRUIT OF A SOPHISTICATED CAPACITY TO RAPIDLY

Allyson Felix leading the successful American team in the 4x400 meters at the Beijing Olympics.

INTRODUCTION Fast to the Finish

TRANSLATE INTENTION INTO ACTION, AS WELL AS A SERIES OF ABILITIES (MOTOR COORDINATION, MOVEMENT CONTROL, RAPIDITY OF INTUITION AND DECISION-MAKING) DERIVING FROM MANY FACTORS. IF WE CLOSELY EXAMINE WHAT A SPRINTER DOES, WE BECOME AWARE THAT ANY SUCCESS DERIVES FROM A DEVELOPED AND TRAINED MUSCULATURE AND OF THE EDUCATION OF MUSCULAR AND MENTAL RESPONSIVENESS ABLE TO PRODUCE THAT 100-M (110-YARD) SPRINT OR 50-M (60-YARD) FREESTYLE SWIMMING RECORD. SPEED IS THEREFORE JUST THE TIP OF AN ICEBERG. WHEN, HOWEVER, WE HAVE TO LOOK BACK INTO THE HISTORY OF SPORT FOR EXAMPLES OF SPEED, ATHLETICS SPRINTERS ALWAYS COME TO

INTRODUCTION Fast to the Finish

MIND. IF THE HISTORY AND GEOGRAPHY OF MALE CHAMPIONS HAS BEEN REWRITTEN OVER THE LAST YEAR, HOMAGE MUST SURELY BE PAID TO SOMEONE WHO 20 YEARS AGO BECAME THE FASTEST WOMAN IN THE WORLD, WHOSE RECORD IS AS YET UNCHAL-LENGED. FLORENCE DELOREZ GRIFFITH-JOYNER, IN 1988 REWROTE THE SPEED AND MEDALS RECORD AT THE SEOUL OLYMPICS, FEEDING UNCONFIRMED SUSPI-CIONS THAT DRUGS WERE BEHIND HER DEVASTATING SUPERIORITY.

SHE STILL HAS NO SUCCESSOR. SHE WOULD NOT ANY-WAY BE ABLE TO NAME ONE AS SHE SUFFERED AN EPILEPTIC FIT IN HER BED IN MISSION VIEJO, IN CALI-FORNIA, IN 1998, A YEAR AFTER RETIRING WHEN SHE

Fast to the Finish

Introduction

WAS JUST 39 YEARS OF AGE. HER 10"49 IN THE 100 M

110 YARDS) AT THE OLYMPIC TRIALS IN INDIANAPOLIS (A

RESULT THAT TODAY WOULD TODAY BE CONSIDERED

AS 'PROBABLY WIND ASSISTED,' BUT WAS THEN AC-

CEPTED AS PERFECTLY LEGITIMATE), HIT A TOP SPEED

OF 40.45 KM/H (25.13 MPH). NO ONE, IN TWENTY YEARS

OF TRYING, HAS YET COME ANYWHERE NEAR THAT.

- Swiss boat Alinghi during the fifth race against New Zealand in the Louis Vuitton
Cup during the 2007 Americas Cup in Valencia.

268-269 ● Second from left, Big Brown, ridden by Kent Desormeaux, leads into a bend during its win in the 134th Kentucky Derby in Louisville on May 3, 2008.

269 ● The mighty haunches of racehorses (Ireland's Pietersen in the foreground) in the fifth race of the Forest Row Stakes at Lingfield, England on July 23, 2008.

Final phase of the second race, the Perri Cuten, of the Caulfield Cup in Melbourne, on October 18, 2008. In the centre and in front is Estee, the eventual winner, ridden by Dwayne Dunn.

A galloping racehorse at the first bend in the 2007 Kentucky Derby in Louisville, won by Street Sense, ridden by Calvin Borel.

The horses land after a fence in the 2008 New Season Steeplechase in Ludlow, one of England's oldest race courses, dating back to the 14th century.

Rimini's Alex De Angelis, who races for San Marino, on a Honda during tests before the 2008 Jerez de la Frontera MotoGP on February 17, 2008.

Spain's Dani Pedroso attacks a bend in the 2008 Assen MotoGP, closely followed by Stoner (Ducati), who eventually beat him to the line.

280 • Rain affects the riders during testing for the 2008 MotoGP at Sachsenring. Rossi is ahead, but ended up losing to Stoner.

281 • Rain in Indianapolis while Valentino Rossi leads into a bend on his Yamaha in practice for the 2008 MotoGP, which he went on to win ahead of Hayden.

282-283 • Synchronized leaning into the bend by Pedrosa, Rossi and Capirossi during the Australian MotoGP on Phillip Island on October 14, 2007, won by Stoner.

284-285 • Practice for the Australian Grand Prix on Phillip Island: American John Hopkins in action on a Suzuki. He finished the race in seventh place.

286-287 • David Coulthard driving for Red Bull in the qualifiers in Monza for the 2008 Italian Formula 1 Grand Prix. The Briton finished 16th.

288 • Queuing in the rain: Australia's Mark Webber drives his Red Bull in the 2008 Italian Formula 1 Grand Prix in Monza. He came seventh in a race won by Vettel in a Toro Rosso

289 • Wet chicanes for Jarno Trulli in a Toyota, leading in the 2008 Italian Formula 1 Grand Prix, in which he finished 13th.

290-291 • Felipe Massa almost slips in the wet in qualifying for the 2008 Italian Formula 1 Grand Prix in Monza: the Brazilian went on to finish in sixth place.

292-293 • It seems like night under the downpour as Lewis Hamilton's McClaren-Mercedes passes by in qualifying for the 2008 Italian Formula 1 Grand Prix in Monza. The British driver finished seventh.

294-295 ● Olivier Panis, who raced with fellow Frenchmen, Nicolas Lapierre and Simon Pagenaud, retiring after nine hours, drives his Matmut Courage Oreca after sunset during qualifying for the 2008 Le Mans 24 Hours.

295 ● Daisuke Itoh's Dome during the qualifiers for the 2008 Le Mans 24 Hours. His team went on to finish last.

296-297 • The Brumos Porsche of Garcia, Donahue, Rice and Law during the Daytona 24 Hours on January 25, 2009, which the team won by overtaking Montoya's Lexus at the finish. The Lexus had dominated the previous three years.

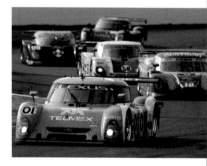

297 • The Chip Ganazzi Lexus of Montoya, Pruett, Rojas and Dixon during the 2009 Daytona 24 Hours.

298-299 ● Mechanics in a frenzy while the Toyota of Kyle Busch is in the pits during 2008 600 NASCAR Sprint Cup in Concord, North Carolina.

300 and 301 ● A car in flames during the Phoenix 500 Mile race of the 2008 NASCAR Sprint Cup: above is Gilliland's Ford, to the right is Jimmie Johnson's Chevrolet.

302-303 and 303 • America's Kyle Burns backfires after his win in the Darlington 500 Miles for the NASCAR Sprint Cup on May 10, 2008 (left) and after his success in the Concord 300 mile race on May 24, 2008 (right).

304-305 • Tony Stewart on a Toyota overtakes Bryan Clauson in the Darlington 200-mile race on May 8, 2008 in the NASCAR Series.

306-307 • A quick pit stop for Kyle Busch in his Toyota during the Darlington 500-mile race for the NASCAR Sprint Cup on May 10, 2008.

308-309 • 2009 Norwegian Rally, first stage: the Citroën Xsara of Petter Solberg and Phillip Mills drives over snow on their way to finishing fifth.

309 • Snow sprays out as the Ford Focus of Henning Solberg and Cato Menkerud drives past in the second stage of the 2009 Norwegian Rally.

310-311 • A long trail of sand and dust left by the Ford Focus of Finland's Mikko Hirvonen and Jarmo Lehtinen in Ngutunui in the 2008 Rally of New Zealand, which saw them finish third, and second in the World Championship.

312 • Norwegians Henning Solberg and Cato Menkerud take a bend on a dirt road in their Ford Focus in the 2008 Turkish Rally.

312-313 • France's Sebastian Loeb, paired with Monacan Daniel Elena, in a Citroën C4 in the mud at the 2008 Argentina Rally in Cordoba.

France's Gilles Panizzi on a Skoda Red Bull at twilight in special testing for the 2006 Montecarlo Rally, descending from Col St. Roch to Lantosque.

316 • A panoramic view over a fence in the third heat of the women's 100 meter hurdles at the 2008 Beijing Games. Australia's McLellan (top) was eventually overtaken by Jamaican Ellis-London, second from bottom.

317 • A clear win for America's Dawn Harper in the final of the 100 meter hurdles at the 2008 Beijing Games. Second-placed Australian, Sally McLellan, is partially obscured, while in the foreground is Canada's Lopes-Schliepp (red vest), in third, with Jamaica's Ennis-London in fifth.

318-319 ● A spectacular picture of the start of the second semifinal of the 100 meters at the 2008 Beijing Games. Jamaica's Asafa Powell (yellow vest, no. 6) went on to win ahead of America's Thompson (to her right) and Martina from the Dutch Antilles (no. 5).

320-321 ● Great Britain's Marilyn Okoro starts the third stage of the final of the 4x400 meters at the 2008 Beijing Games, in which Britain finished fifth.

First heat of the 400 meter hurdles at the 2007 World Athletics Championships in Osaka: America's Tiffany Ross-Williams leads ahead of Kazakhstan's Tatyana Azarova (629) and Ukraine's Anastasiya Rabchenyuk (926), who was eliminated. Ross-Williams finished seventh in the final.

324 ● America's Lauryn Williams, during the semifinal of the 100 meters at the 2008 Beijing Games in which she finished third.

324-325 ● American Walter Dix sets off at the start of his 200 meter heat at the 2008 Beijing Games, in which he finished second. He won the bronze medal in the final.

326 • Final phase of a quarter final of the 100 meters at the 2008 Beijing Games. From left Nigeria's Olusoji Fasuba (fourth and eliminated), America's Tyson Gay, second, and Colombia's Daniel Grueso, who finished last.

327 • Powerful running by US decathlete Bryan Clay in the 100 meters during the decathlon at the 2006 US Championships in Indianapolis.

328-329 • Finalists start from the blocks in the 100 meter final at the 2008 Beijing Games. Number 4 is worn by the Jamaican winner Usain Bolt, 5 by Trinidad's Richard Thompson, who took silver, and 6 by America's Walter Dix, who won bronze.

2006 AT&T USA OUTDOOR
TRACK & FIELD CHAMPIONSHIPS

B. Clay

330 • German decathlete Jan Felix Knobel in the 110 meter hurdles in the decathlon at the 2008 World Junior Athletics Championship in Bydgoszcz, Poland.

330-331 • Final hurdle of a 100 meter semifinal at the 2008 Beijing Games. On the right is the eventual winner, Cuban Dayron Robles with a clear lead, on the left is second-placed American David Payne, and in the center is France's Ladji Doucoure, third.

332 • Swiss Simon Amman in the ski-jump trial at the Ski Jumping World Cup on 6 January in Bischofshofen in Germany.

333 • Swiss Guido Landert about to take-off from the ski jump in the team trial for the World Ski Jumping Championship on February 24, 2008 at Oberstdorf in Austria.

334-335 • Slovenia's Alex Gorza rounds a gate during the SuperG at the 2008-09 World Cup on December 6, 2008 in Beaver Creek. Gorza went on to finish ninth.

336-337 • Sestriere, February 17, 2006, the Turin Winter Games: the Czech Republic's Lucie Hrstkova during the slalom in which she finished 40th after the first leg, and was eliminated in the second.

337 • American Lindsey Vonn-Kildow flies over a hump in the SuperG of the Alpine Skiing World Championships in Are, Sweden, in which she took silver.

338-339 • Miraculous balancing by France's Jean-Baptiste Grange during the giant slalom at the 2008 World Cup in Val d'Isère, in which he finished 16th.

340-341 • Russia's Dmitry Vasilyev has just taken off from the ski jump at Liberec in the Czech Republic during the 2009 World Nordic Ski Championships. The strong wind limited the competition to one jump, in which Vasilyev finished seventh.

● Poland's Kamil Stach training before the World Cup skeleton match on January 24, 2009 in Whistler, Canada.

344 • A panoramic view of the track at Whistler during training for the
2009 Skeleton World Cup.

345 • Germany's Marion Trott competing during the 2008 Skeleton World
Championships in Altenberg, Germany.

346 • The four-man bobsleigh driven by Matthias Höpfner during the start of a descent in the Bobsleigh World Championships at Altenberg, Germany.

347 • The French bobsleigh driven by Bruno Mingeon in action during the final of the four-man bobsleigh at the Turin Winter Games.

An acrobatic bend in the final of the 100 meters at the World Short Track Speed Skating Championships in Gangneng in South Korea on March 9, 2008. South Korea's Lee Ho-suk is in the lead and would go on to win gold.

350 • Japan's Hirako, Dejima and Sugmimora accelerate in the team pursuit trial at the World Speed Skating Championships at Nagano, Japan.

351 • America's Eli Ochowicz in the 500 meters at the World Speed Skating Championships at Nagano, Japan.

352 ● Holland's Kramer, Heuvel and Wennemars during the team pursuit trial at the 2008 World Speed Skating Championships.

352-353 ● Italy's Enrico Fabris during the 5000 Herenveen, Holland, during the 2009 European Speed Skating Championships.

354 • America's David Zabriskie about to take seventh place in the prologue to the 2008 Tour of California at Palo Alto.

355 • A determined grimace from Luxembourg's Kim Kirchen while he crosses the line of the 19th stage of the 2007 Tour de France, a time trial from Cognac to Angoulême.

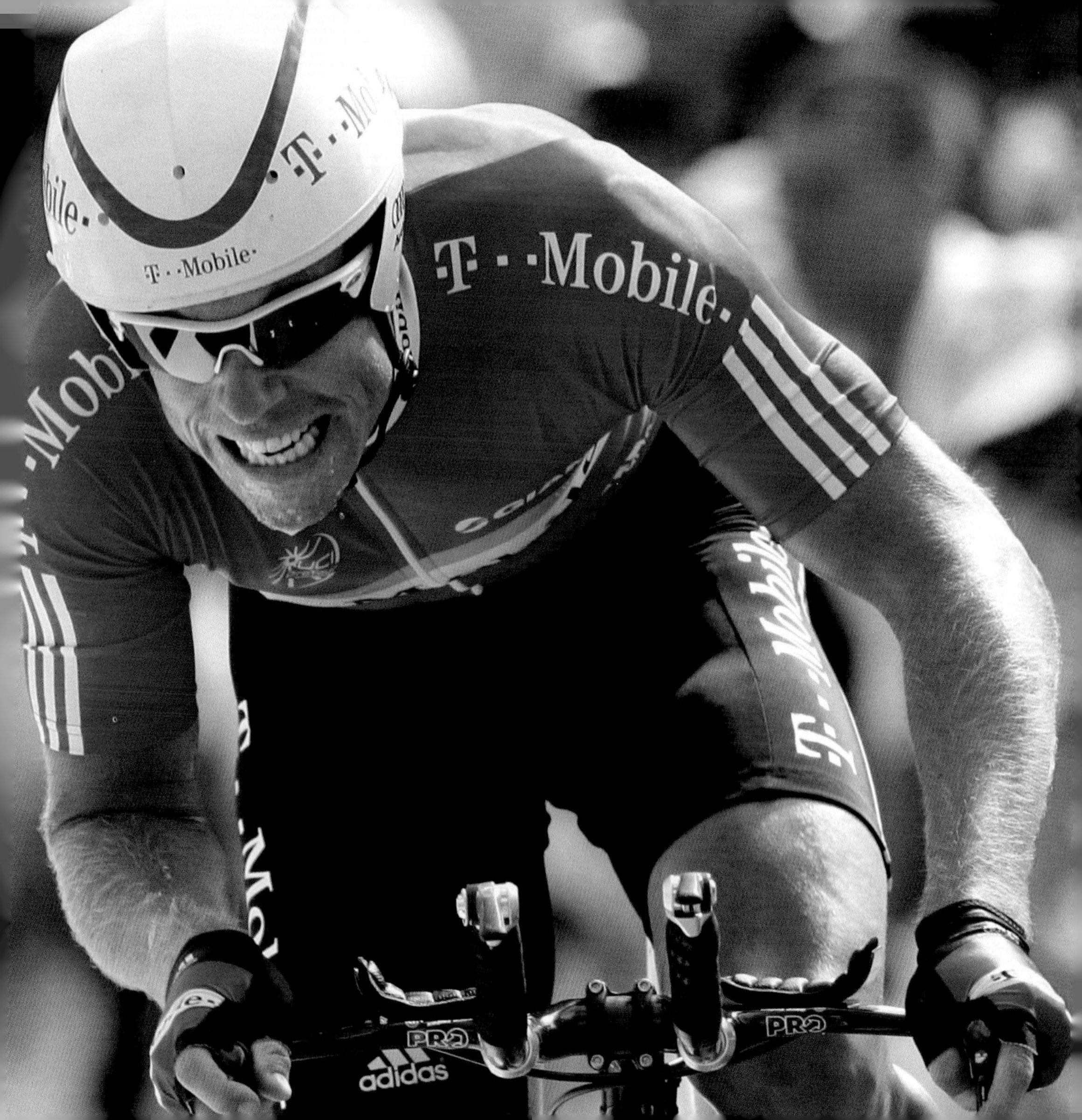
T · · Mobile ·
T · ·Mobile·
adidas
PRO

356 ● America's Lance Armstrong in the prologue to the 2009 Tour of California in Sacramento on 14 February.

357 ● America's Mike Creed in the fifth stage of the 2008 Tour of California, in a time trial on the Solvang track.

358-359 ● Group sprint in the fifth stage of the 2008 Tour de France, from Cholet to Chateauroux. The winner was Britain's Mark Cavendish, on the left in a blue vest, with his first win of the Tour.

359 ● Norway's Edval Boasson Hagel beats Italy's Giairo Ermeti on the last bend to win the fourth stage of the Tour of Great Britain in Stoke-on-Trent.

359

360 ● The German team in action in the team pursuit at the 2009 Track Cycling World Cup in Copenhagen.

361 ● Copenhagen, February 13, 2009; France's Clara Sanchez overtakes Ukraine's Lyobov Shulika on a bend at the 2009 Track Cycling World Cup.

362-363 ● The British pursuit team in action during the qualifiers for the 2009 Track Cycling World Cup in Copenhagen. Ed Clancy, World and Olympic team champion, is in second place.

364-365 • New Zealand's Aaaron McIntosh and Mark Kennedy in their Tornado at the 2008 World Championships in Takapuna, New Zealand. They finished twelfth.

366 • Luna Rossa catches the wind in the seventh Oracle race during the Pacific Series of the Louis Vuitton Cup, during the Americas Cup at Waitemata on February 5, 2009.

367 • Bernard Labro at work while Luna Rossa completes one side of the triangle of the regatta in race 7 of the Pacific Series of the Americas Cup at Waitemata.

368-369 • Damiani Italia Challenge bowman, Matteo Auguadro, at work in race 7 against New Zealand in the Pacific Series of the 2009 Americas Cup.

370-371 • Puma and its crew in action one week into the first stage of the 2008-09 Ocean Race from Alicante to Cape Town, on October 11, 2008, with ten stages and eight boats starting.

371 • Picture from on high of the Delta Lloyd at the start of the third stage of the 2008-09 Ocean Race, from Cochin in India to Singapore.

372 • Alinghi during the fifth race of the 2007 Americas Cup in Valencia, Spain.

373 • New Zealand raises the spinnaker during the fifth race against Alinghi.

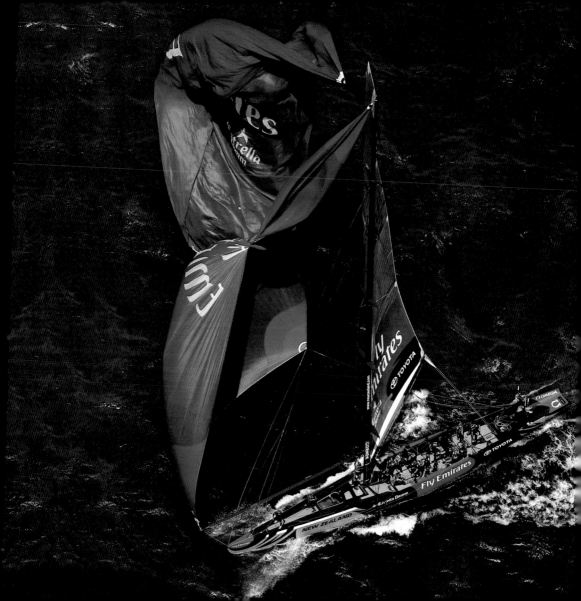

374 ● Bryony Shaw racing in the RS-X class at the 2008 Beijing Games: she won the bronze medal.

374-375 ● Federico Esposito racing during the third day of the RS-X class at the 2008 World Championship in Takapuna, New Zealand.

376-377 ● 2008 Beijing Games, RS-X sailboard trial: American Ben Barger is in action. He went on to finish 26th.

ACCURACY and CONCENTRATION

- Germany's Erik Zabel is a picture of concentration before the start of the German road cycling championships in Wiesbaden on July 1, 2007.

INTRODUCTION Accuracy and Concentration

A CONCENTRATED PERSON IS OFTEN AN AC-CURATE PERSON, BOTH IN SPORT AND IN LIFE. THIS SORT OF FRIGHTENING AND INFALLIBLE ACCURACY IS OFTEN OWED TO AN ABILITY TO CONCENTRATE IN THE PRESENT MOMENT.

IT IS UNUSUAL FOR THE TWO TALENTS TO BE SEPA-RATE. THERE CAN BE THE BORDERLINE CASE OF IN-CREDIBLE AND UNEXPECTED ACCURACY ARISING OUT OF A DESPERATE ACTION, A LAST THROW OF THE DICE DICTATED BY THE NEED TO CATCH AN OPPONENT. THERE HAVE BEEN VARIOUS CASES OF THIS IN BAS-KETBALL, WHEN A LONG DISTANCE THROW, OR ONE

- Tiger Woods considers his strategy before a putt at the fourth play-off hole during the 108th US Open in San Diego on June 16, 2008.

INTRODUCTION Accuracy and Concentration

MADE IN VERY DIFFICULT CONDITIONS, HITS THE TARGET. ASIDE FROM A NUMBER OF LUCKY CASES, JERRY WEST IS OFTEN MENTIONED AS AN EXAMPLE OF ACCURACY IN A HOPELESS SITUATION, WHEN IN 1970 HE SCORED FROM 59 FT (18 M), THREE SECONDS FROM TIME DURING THE THIRD OF SEVEN NBA FINAL PLAY-OFFS BETWEEN HIS LOS ANGELES LAKERS AND THE NEW YORK KNICKERBOCKERS. TWO POINTS BEHIND, WEST SCORED AN INCREDIBLE BASKET TO SQUARE THE MATCH, WHICH THE TEAM THEN WON IN EXTRA TIME.

HOWEVER, THIS IS VERY MUCH THE EXCEPTION. A FOOTBALL PENALTY IS THE MOST COMMON SITUATION WHERE ACCURACY AND CONCENTRATION LITERALLY SQUARE UP TO EACH OTHER. THE PENALTY TAKER RE-

INTRODUCTION Accuracy and Concentration

QUIRES ACCURACY AND CONCENTRATION AT THE SAME TIME AND TO THE SAME DEGREE, WHILE THE GOALKEEPER DEFINITELY NEEDS THE LATTER, BUT FOR HIM IT IS MORE A MATTER OF GUESSING WHICH WAY TO DIVE.

IN THIS EXAMPLE, WE SEE TWO PLAYERS WHO ODDLY ENOUGH SHARE THE SAME SURNAME, MORO, EVEN THOUGH THEY ARE UNRELATED. GIUSEPPE MORO HOLDS THE RECORD FOR THE MOST PENALTIES SAVED, WHILE ADELIO MORO HOLDS THAT FOR THE MOST PENALTIES SCORED IN SERIE A. THE FORMER WAS TORINO'S YOUNG GOALKEEPER FOLLOWING THE SUPERGRA TRAGEDY, WHO SAVED 16 PENALTIES OUT OF 44 IN THE 1949-50 SEASON. ANOTHER 7 WENT

Accuracy and Concentration

Introduction

WIDE AND ONE HIT THE POST. THE LATTER PLAYER HOLDS THE RECORD OF ALWAYS HAVING SUCCESSFULLY SCORED FROM THE SPOT.

ADELIO MORO PLAYED IN MIDFIELD FOR VARIOUS TEAMS, INCLUDING INTER AND A.C. MILAN, SCORING 10 OUT OF 10 IN HIS CAREER. THEY NEVER FACED EACH OTHER, BUT IT WOULD HAVE BEEN GREAT TO FIND OUT WHICH MORO WAS THE MOST ACCURATE AND MOST CONCENTRATED.

- Shaquille O'Neal of the Phoenix Suns prepares himself in an NBA away match against the Toronto Raptors on January 18, 2009.

386 • Indian cricketer Anil Kumble batting during the second day of the third Test between India and Australia on October 30, 2008.

387 • Australia's Nathan Hauritz prepares to bowl during a training session for the Australian cricket team in Adelaide on November 27, 2008.

388 • Pittsburgh Pirates' receiver Ronny Paulino waiting for the ball in a pre-season training match against the Toronto Blue Jays in Bradenton, Florida, on March 17, 2008.

389 • Ervin Santana of the Los Angeles Angels is ready to pitch from the mound against the Chicago Cubs in a pre-season match, on March 14, 2008, at Mesa, Arizona.

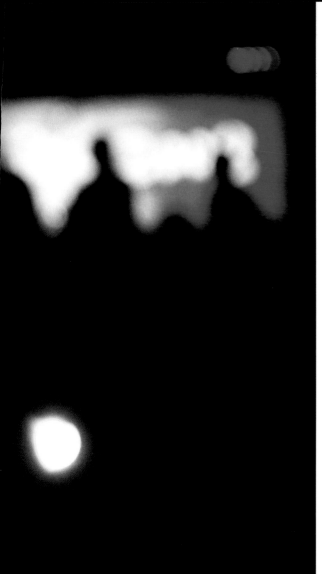

• Poland's Rafa Kaczor is deep in concentration as he prepares to fight Kazakhstan's Mirat Sarsembayev in the first round of the 51 kg class at the 2008 Beijing Games, which he went on to lose on points.

● Alfondo Boone of the Kansas City Chiefs, preparing to take the field against the Buffalo Bills in the NFL match played in Kansas City on November 23, 2008.

394 • Wales' Sion E. Bebb considers his line of stroke on the 17th hole of the second round of the Portuguese Masters in Vilamoura on October 17, 2008.

395 • Columbia's Camilo Villegas ponders his best strategy before hitting the ball at the 15th hole of the first round of the BMW golf tournament at St Louis, Missouri, on September 5, 2008.

396 • Basketballer Michael Jordan playing golf during a Pro-Am on May 2, 2007 at Charlotte, North Carolina.

396-397 • Northern Ireland's Graeme McDowell in action at the second hole in the first round of the Volvo Masters at Sotogrande, Spain on October 31, 2008.

398-399 ● Atlanta, September 28, 2008: Camilo Vilegas carefully decides the best strategy to adopt in the East Lake tournament.

400-401 ● Tiger Woods checks the likely trajectory before hitting a ball at the Ritz-Carlton Club tournament at Dove Mountain, in Marana, Arizona, on February 26, 2009.

● Norway's Olaf Tufte
concentrates before
the start of his singles
heat at the Rowing
World Cup on June 1,
2007 in Ottensheim,
Austria.

Preparation rituals for British sprinter Mark Lewis-Francis on the blocks in his 100 meter heat at the 2006 European Games in Gothenburg, Sweden.

406-407 • Canada's Denny Morrison awaits the gun at the starting line of his 1500 meter heat in the 2007-08 Speed Skating World Cup at Heerenveen in Holland.

407 • Norwegian Hege Bokko ready to start the 500 meter race at the 2009 European Championships in Heerenveen, Holland.

408 • German cyclist Ronny Scholz adjusts his glasses before the road race at the 2006 World Championships in Salzburg.

409 • Australian Cadel Evans gets ready at the start of the last stage of the 2008 Tour de France, the time trial from Cerilly to Saint-Amand-Montrond.

410 • Welshman James Hook of the Ospreys takes extreme care in positioning the ball before taking a penalty against Worcester Warriors in the Energy Cup in Swansea on October 26, 2008.

411 • Alessandro del Piero takes stock of the situation before a free kick against Fiorentina in the championship match on January 24, 2009 in Turin.

412-413 • Calgary Flames goalkeeper Miikka Kiprusoff prepares for the start of the match against the Nashville Predators in the 2007-08 NHL season game in Edmonton on March 7, 2008.

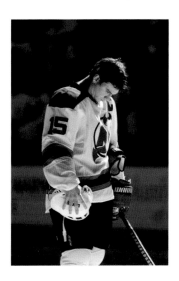

413 • Jamie Langenbrunner of the New Jersey Devils listens to the US national anthem with his head bowed before the start of the NHL match against the Columbus Blue Jackets on January 16, 2009 in Columbus.

414 ● Britain's Lewis Hamilton concentrates before climbing into his McClaren-Mercedes on the starting grid of the 2008 German Formula 1 Grand Prix in Hockenheim.

415 ● Germany's Silke Kraushaar-Pielach in a curious posture before the start of the 2008 World Luge Championships in Oberhof, Germany.

416-417 ● American Sadam Ali, born in Brooklyn but of Yemeni origin, is thoughtful as he enters the ring for a fight against Romania's Georgian Popescu in the first round of the 60 kg class at the 2008 Beijing Games. He was soundly beaten on points.

418 ● Ukraine's Wladimir Klitschko awaits the start of his successful defense of his IBO and IBF world heavyweight title against America's Lamon Brewster in Cologne on July 7, 2007.

419 ● Captain of the junior All Blacks, Corey Flynn, shows his determination before the start of the match against the Samoan juniors in the 2006 'Pacific 5' in Auckland, New Zealand.

420 • El Salvador's Eva Dimas
thanks the public (and herself)
after a successful lift in the 75 kg
class at the 2007 Pan American
Games in Rio.

420-421 • Italy's Moreno Boer
prepares for a lift in the 105 kg
weightlifting competition
at the 2008 Beijing Games:
she finished 18th.

422 • Malaysian diver Leong Mun Yee during the preliminaries on the three-meter springboard at the 2008 Beijing Games in which she finished 21st.

423 • Italian diver Tania Cagnotto ready to perform a dive in the preliminaries for the three-meter springboard at the 2008 Beijing Games in which she finished fifth.

● A bit of stretching for America's Michael Phelps before the 200 meter butterfly semifinal at the 2008 Beijing Games.

Total concentration for Germany's Britta Steffen before her 50 meter freestyle heat at the 2008 German Championships in Berlin.

Croatian water polo players make their last preparations before the match against Hungary in the 2007 World Championships in Melbourne, which they won 9-8 to take gold.

430 • Austria's Daniel Lackner arranges his helmet before the ski jump at the 2009 Nordic Skiing World Cup at Bischofshofen.

431 • Australia's Amy Hetzel puts on her cap ahead of a qualifier against Greece at the 2008 Beijing Games, won by Australia 12-8. Greece gained their revenge with a 9-8 win in the match for seventh place.

432 • America's Kerron Clement places her hands on the track for the start of the 400 meter hurdles semifinal at the 2008 Beijing Games.

432-433 • France's Martinica Phara Anacharsis prepares herself at the start of the first stage of a 4x400 meter semifinal at the 2008 Beijing Games. France missed out on the final.

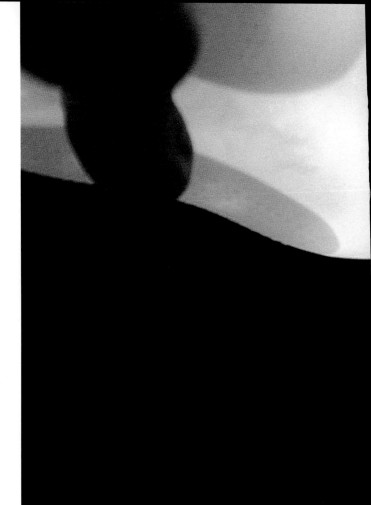

● Cuba's Yankiel León Alarcon receives assistance in the corner during the bantamweight final against Mongolia Badar Uugan Enkhbatyn, who lost on points, at the 2008 Beijing Games.

436 • Germany's Fabian Hambüchen finishes his bandaging before the first round of the gymnastics final at the 2008 Beijing Games.

437 • A gymnast dries their hands for a firmer grip during the individual competition at the 2008 Beijing Games.

438-439 • Russia's Ivan Skobryov concentrates before the start of the 1500 meter heat in the 2007-08 Speed skating World Cup trial at Heerenveen in Holland.

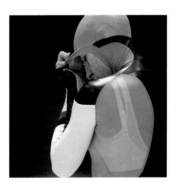

439 • Germany's Anni Friesinger arranges her hair under her cap before the start of the 1000 meter final at the 2006-07 Speed skating World Cup trial at Heerenveen.

440 • Russia's Dinara Safina, Marat's younger sister, receives a ball for service in the third round of the 2009 Australian Open against Estonian Kaia Kanepi.

441 • Sweden's Carolina Kluft prepares to put the shot in the heptathlon in the European Championships in Gothenburg, Sweden.

442 • Arizona Cardinals Dominique Rodgers-Cromartie and Michael Adams pray before the match against the Pittsburg Steelers in the 2009 Super Bowl in Tampa.

443 • Moran Norris of the San Francisco 49ers concentrates his mind in the dressing room ahead of an NFL match against the Oakland Raiders in San Francisco on October 8, 2006, which the 49ers won 34-20.

444 • Curious service posture by Sweden's Jörgen Persson during his semifinal against China's Ma Lin in the table tennis singles at the 2008 Beijing Games. He went on to lose in five sets.

445 • The ball soars over the face of China's Wang Hao while he serves against his compatriot Ma Lin in the table tennis singles final at the 2008 Beijing Games, in which he won gold.

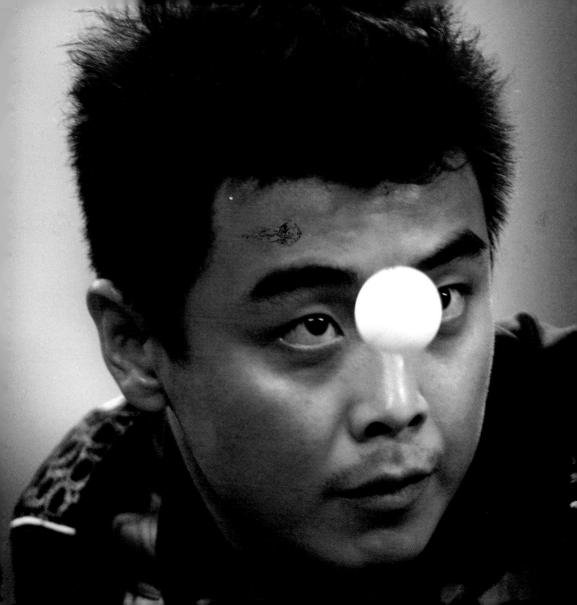

Two phases of the run-up by American Allison Stokke, who became an Internet sex symbol during the pole vault qualifiers at the 2007 US Juniors Championship in Indianapolis (above) and in the seniors the same year (right).

448 ● The Alinghi crew working during a race against New Zealand in the 2007 Americas Cup.

448-449 ● Wild Oats XI bowman Sven Ruenow fixes the spinnaker during the maxi-yacht race on December 16, 2008 in Sydney, which the boat went on to win ahead of 16 others.

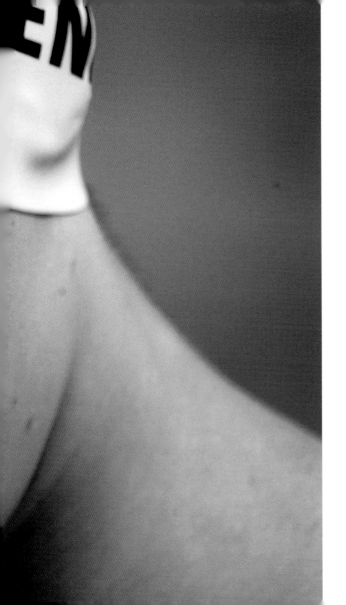

America's Mary Descenza prepares for her heat of the 100 meter freestyle at the 2006 US Championships in Irvine, California.

The start of a semifinal of the 50 meter freestyle at the 2007 World Championships in Melbourne: Australia's Libby Lenton in the foreground.

454 ● Close-up of a gymnast's toe support at the 2008 Beijing Games.

455 ● A gymnast's feet on the beam during the qualifiers at the 2008 Beijing Games.

● Calais Campbell of the Arizona Cardinals in deep concentration before the 2009 Super Bowl against the Pittsburgh Steelers in Tampa, which the Cardinals lost 23-27.

458 • Dominica's Félix Sanchez praying before a 400 meter hurdles heat at the 2008 Beijing Games.

458-459 • Before the start of the semifinal of the 100 meters at the 2008 Beijing Games, Jamaica's Usain Bolt, the fastest runner in 2008, looks up for support.

460-461 • Italian Super Heavyweight Roberto Cammarelle about to climb into the ring before his victorious boxing final against China's Zhang Zhilei at the 2008 Beijing Games.

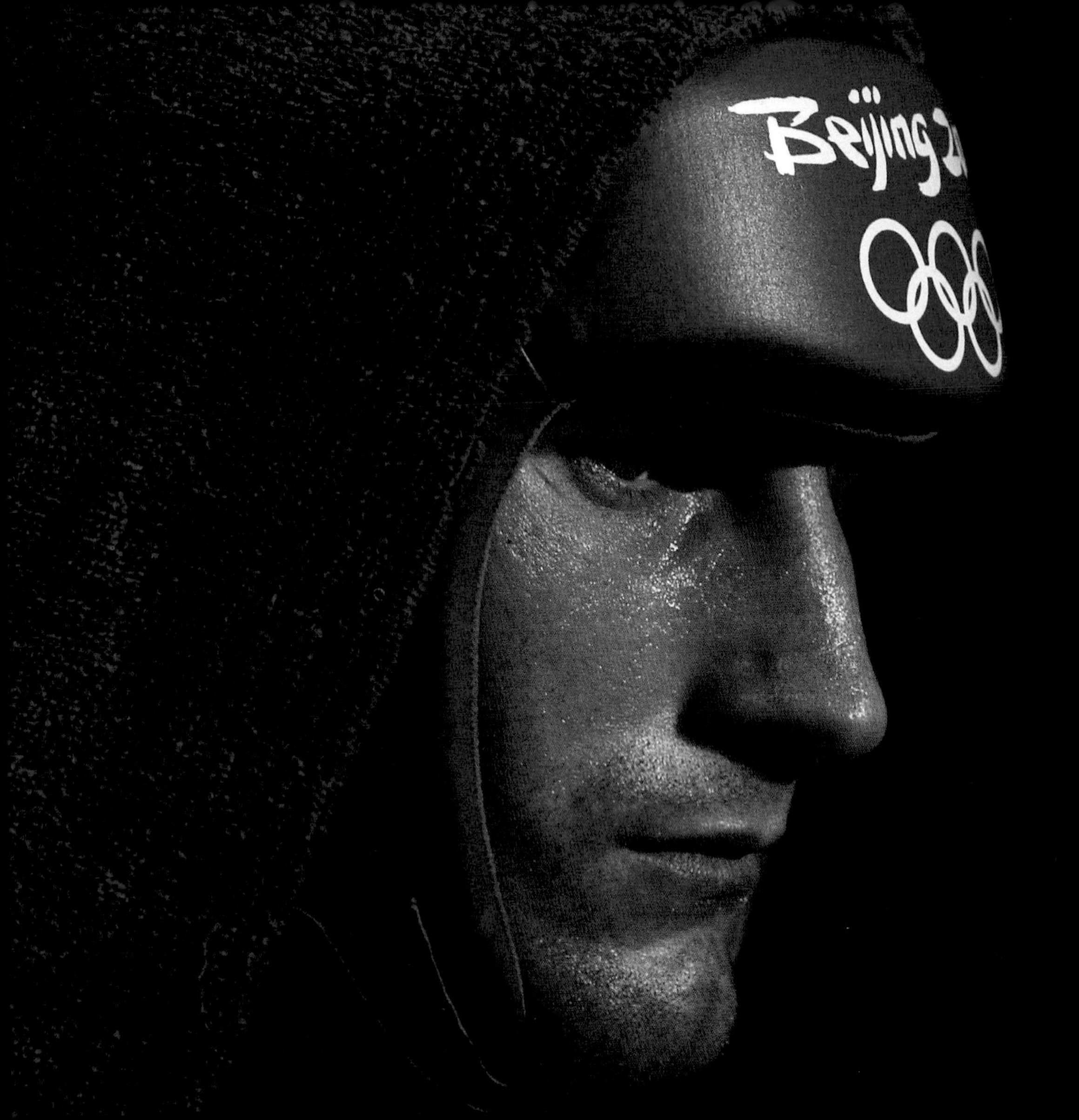
Beijing

Croatia's Jospi Pavic
glances at his team-
mates in a break in the
water polo final against
Hungary at the 2007
World Championships
in Melbourne.

464 • The concentration of Venus Williams as she prepares to return serve against Japan's Akiko Morigami at Wimbledon 2007.

465 • Japan's Kei Nishikori serving against France's Marc Gicquel in the first round at Wimbledon 2008.

466-467 ● Spain's Rafael Nadal hits a shot in his match against compatriot Feliciano Lopez in the quarterfinals of the 2008 Madrid Masters.

467 ● A serve by Czech Tomas Berdych in the semifinal against Serb Novak Djokovic in the 2008 Thailand Open.

● Britain's Linzi Snow
prepares for the start
of the 800 meters,
which she won, at the
2007 Glasgow
Grand Prix.

470 • Ferrari's Felipe Massa driving during practice for the 2008 Silverstone Formula 1 Grand Prix.

471 • Germany's Kristan Bromley in action during the 2008 Skeleton World Championships in Altenberg, Germany.

472 • Alfred Aboya of the UCLA Bruins eyes the basket before a free throw against the Oregon State Beavers in the quarterfinals of basketball's 2006 'Pacific 10' in Los Angeles.

473 • Carolina Panthers receiver, Dwayne Jarrett, collects a play during the warm-up before the NFL 2007-08 season match against the Tampa Bay Buccaneers in Tampa that the Panthers won 31-23.

474 • Close-up of a player who has stopped the ball on the scrimmage line that marks the attack and defense zones in American football.

474-475 • Marshawn Lynch, Buffalo Bills running back, running with the ball to his chest against the Philadelphia Eagles (who won 17-9) in a 2007-08 NFL game in Philadelphia.

476 • Australia's Michael Brown shooting in the Rifle 3 Position (Pairs) at the
2006 Commonwealth Games.

477 • Brown's team-mate, Ben Burge, during the same competition. The pair won silver.

478 ● China's Du Ling, who went on to be Olympic champion in this discipline,
during the 50 meter rifle at the 2008 Beijing Games.

479 ● Great Britain's Louise Minett aims at the target during the final of the 3 position
rifle (pairs) at the 2006 Commonwealth Games, in which she won gold for England
alongside Becky Spicer.

480-481 ● China's Liu Yingzi blows into the rifle's barrel after a shot in the trap shooting qualifiers at the 2008 Beijing Games.

481 ● 2008 Beijing Games, skeet competition: China's Wei Ning discharges her weapon.

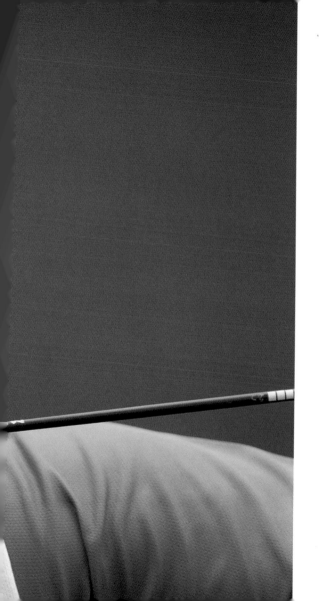

● Italy's Mauro Nespolli (left) draws his bow during the team trial at the 2008 Beijing Games in which he won silver with Di Buò and Galiazzo.

484 ● Turkey's Zekiye Keskin Satir lets off an arrow during the individual archery competition at the 2008 Beijing Games.

485 ● South Korea's Yun Ok-Hee during the battle for bronze in the individual archery competition at the 2008 Beijing Games, which he won against North Korea's Kwon Un-Sil.

486 • Curling, US 2009 Olympic trials at Broomfield, Colorado: in action is John Shuster, the bronze medal winner in Turin 2006.

487 • Great Britain's David Murdoch throws his stone during the curling match against the USA at the 2006 Turin Winter Olympics, which GB lost 8-9.

Great Britain's Ewan McDonald decides his strategy before throwing his stone in the USA-GB curling match at Turin 2006: the USA won 9-8 to take the bronze.

USA Olympic trials at Broomfield, Colorado, February 27, 2009: in action is America's Courtney George, eighth at Turin 2006.

HARMONY in MOVEMENT

- Italy's Carolina Kostner in action during the short program at the figure skating international competition in Ottawa, Canada in 2008.

INTRODUCTION Harmony in Movement

GRACE AND ELEGANCE ARE CERTAINLY NOT PREROGATIVES LIMITED TO WOMEN IN SPORT. ON THE CONTRARY, GRACE IS OFTEN ASSOCIATED WITH MALE DISCIPLINES. JUST CONSIDER A DIVE, EVEN A FAIRLY STRAIGHTFORWARD ONE, WHICH OOZES GRACE AND ELEGANCE AT ONE AND THE SAME TIME. ONE COULD SAY THAT GRACE AND ELEGANCE ARE INNATE QUALITIES AND THAT WE HAVE A NATURAL PROPENSITY TO EXPRESS THEM.

HOWEVER, IN FACT WE HAVE KNOWN FOR SOME TIME THAT THEY, LIKE DEFTNESS, BALANCE, AND SENSE OF RHYTHM, ARE NOT NECESSARILY INNATE AND THAT AN

• Japan's Kohhei Kudok in competition in the halfpipe at the Snowboard World Cup in Wanaka, New Zealand, on September 6, 2008.

INTRODUCTION Harmony in Movement

ATHLETE NEEDS TO TRAIN MORE OR LESS FROM BIRTH TO BE ABLE PUT IN THAT PERFECT PERFORMANCE FOR A JURY. HOWEVER, WE DO USUALLY ASSOCIATE THESE NOTIONS WITH WOMEN'S SPORTS. WHEN KORBUT AND COMANECI BURST ONTO THE SCENE AND BEFORE THE SERIOUS CONCERNS ABOUT THE AGE AND DEVELOPMENT OF GIRLS, OF GIRL-GYMNASTS, THE WORLD WAS BOWLED OVER AND CAPTIVATED BY TWO GIRLS WHO GAVE THE SORT OF GREAT PERFORMANCES THAT HAD PREVIOUSLY ONLY BEEN SEEN FROM MATURE AND FULLY FORMED WOMEN.

THE SOVIET OLGA KORBUT, 'THE BABY SPARROW,' BORN IN BELARUS IN 1955, ENCHANTED SPECTATORS

INTRODUCTION Harmony in Movement

AT THE 1972 MUNICH GAMES WITH HER SMILE AND THE TINY GRACE OF HER FIGURE, AS WELL AS WITH A NUMBER OF EXTRAORDINARY EXERCISES PERFORMED FOR THE FIRST TIME, SUCH AS THE DEATH-DEFYING BACK FLIP ON THE BEAM AND THEN ON THE ASYMMETRIC/PARALLEL BARS, IN THE COURSE IN DOING WHICH SHE WON OVER THE JURIES. THE PUBLIC APPRECIATED THE GOLDEN GIRL, THE JUDGES HER ACROBATICS. SHE WON THREE GOLDS AND A SILVER IN HER OLYMPIC DÉBUT.

ELEGANCE IS ALSO THE CRITERION BY WHICH FIGURE SKATING IS MEASURED. MEN AND WOMEN COMPETE IN THEIR OWN CATEGORIES, BUT ONE WOMAN ALONE, THE BRITON MADGE SYERS, BEAT EVERY MAN BAR

Harmony in Movement

Introduction

ONE IN THE 1902 WORLD CHAMPIONSHIPS FIGURE SKATING COMPETITION BEFORE THE INTERNATIONAL FEDERATION SEPARATED MEN AND WOMEN. SWEDISH GOLD-MEDAL WINNER ULRICH SALCHOW ALSO PAID A GRACIOUS AND ELEGANT TRIBUTE TO HER AT THOSE GAMES, ASKING HER TO STAND AT THE TOP OF THE PODIUM, HAVING COME SECOND, DEFEATING ALL THE OTHER MEN. HE ALSO GAVE HER HIS MEDAL.

- The Santa Clara Aquamaids during the team routine at the
US Synchronized Swimming Championships on April 26, 2007 in Indianapolis.

500 ● Americans Jane Summersett and Todd Gilles in the free dance competition at the 2009 US Figure Skating Championships on January 24, in Cleveland, Ohio.

501 ● France's Pernelle Carron and Mathieu Jost in the free dance during Skate America 2008 on October 26, at Everett, Washington.

502 • Finland's Laura Lepisto in the free dance at the ISU Grand Prix on November 29, 2008 in Tokyo.

503 • Japan's Daisuke Takahashi during the 2008 Japan Open Figure Skating Competition in Saitama.

504 • Annette Dytrt, a German of Czech origin, touches her head with her skate during her free dance at the 2009 European Figure Skating Championships in Helsinki, Finland.

505 • Canada's Mira Leung grabs a skate with her hands during the short program at Skate America 2008 at Everett, Washington.

Japan's Mirai Nagasu in a spin during the short program (above) and during another elegant move (right) at the US Open 2009 in Cleveland, Ohio.

508 • Russia's Yevgeniya Kanayeva performing in the hoop during the individual rhythmic competition at the 2008 Beijing Games, in which she won gold.

509 • Malaysia's Elaine Tan performs with the ribbons during the team competition at the Australian Youth Olympic Festival in Sydney in January of 2007.

510-511 • Three of the five Bulgarians competing with the hoops during the team rhythmic gymnastics competition at the 2008 Beijing Games. Bulgaria finished fifth.

512 • Russia's Yevgeniya Kanayeva with the clubs during the individual rhythmic competition at the 2008 Beijing Games. She went on to win gold.

513 • Byelorussia's Lyubov Cherkasina in the ribbon competition at the 2008 Beijing Games. She did not progress beyond the first round.

514-515 ● The tape comes alive, twirled by South Africa's Odette Richard during the preliminaries of the individual rhythmic competition at the 2008 Beijing Games, where she came second to last.

516-517 ● A hoop jump performed by a participant at the US rhythmic gymnastics Olympic trials in Philadelphia on May 20, 2008. No American women made it to the Games.

518 ● China's Wu Jiaqui performs with the ball in the rhythmic dance at the Australian Youth Olympic Festival in Sydney in 2007.

519 ● Israel's Irina Risenzon on the rope during the final of the individual rhythmic competition at the 2008 Beijing Games. She finished ninth.

520 • Romania's Sandra Izbasa finishes her floor exercise at the 2008 Beijing Games, where she won gold.

520-521 • Russia's Anna Pavlova on the beam in the gymnastics at the 2008 Beijing Games, in which she finished fourth.

522 • America's Bridget Sloan in the floor exercise in the team competition at the 2008 Beijing Games.

523 • Moscow-born American Nastia Liukin 'flies' during the team competition at the 2008 Beijing Games, in which the US won silver.

America's Alicia Sacramone kisses the beam during the team gymnastic competition at the 2008 Beijing Games, where the USA finished second.

526-527 • China's Yuyuan Jiang smiles at the end of her floor exercise at the 2008 Beijing Games. She went on to finish fourth.

527 • China's Li Shanshan on the beam at the 2008 Beijing Games. She came sixth in the individual competition.

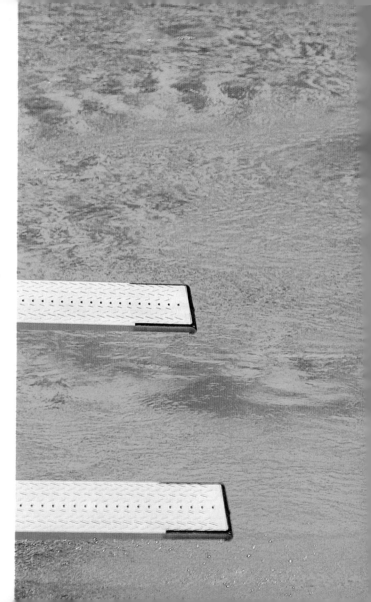

China's Wang Feng, diving off the one-meter board at the 2005 Montreal World Championships competition. He won gold in the two-meter competition.

530 • A synchronized dive at the 2006 Commonwealth Games in Melbourne: Malaysia's James Sandayud and Bryan Nickson in action.

531 • Synchronized diving at the 2008 Beijing Games: a cross by Americans Chris Colwill and Jevon Tarantino, who went on to finish fourth.

532-533 • Japanese diver Mai Nakagawa from the 10-meter springboard at the 2008 Beijing Games, in which she finished eleventh.

534-535 • France's Marc Boblet on Whitni Star during the dressage World Cup on December 17, 2008 in London. He finished seventh.

535 • Sweden's Minna Telde rides Don Charly at the dressage World Cup on December 17, 2008 in London. Telde came fifth.

536 ● Britain's Michael Whitaker, three-time European Champion, Olympic and World silver medalist, rides Cover Girl in the show-jumping competition at Hickstead on July 27, 2008.

537 ● Show-jumping at Hickstead in the George V Cup. Germany's Philipp Weisshaupt clears the water jump on Leoville.

Grey Abbey, ridden by Graham Lee, jumps a fence and sets off for the next one at the Betfair Steeplechase Cup at Aintree in April of 2005.

Thoroughbreds reflected in the water jump during the Cheltenham Royal Steeplechase in March of 2007.

542 • A star performed by the US team at the 2008 Beijing Games.

543 • Russians performing a ballet leg double during the synchronized freestyle exercise at the 2008 Beijing Games.

544-545 • The US synchronized swimming team at the 2008 Beijing Games perform a combined spin. They finished fifth.

546-547 • The Japanese team jump out of the water during the synchronized swimming competition at the 2008 Beijing Games, where they finished sixth.

548 • An Egyptian performs a back-flip during the team synchronized swimming competition at the 2007 World Swimming Championship in Melbourne.

549 • A Japanese swimmer flies through the air at the 2007 World Swimming Championship in Melbourne.

Australian surfer Tom Whitaker rides the waves of Hawaii in the 2008 Triple Crown on the north coast of Oahu island.

552 • Portugal's Tiago Pires about to win the professional surfers' World Tour series in Tahiti in 2008.

553 • Hawaii's Megan Abubo during a pause in the World Tour pro 2008 in Torquay, Australia.

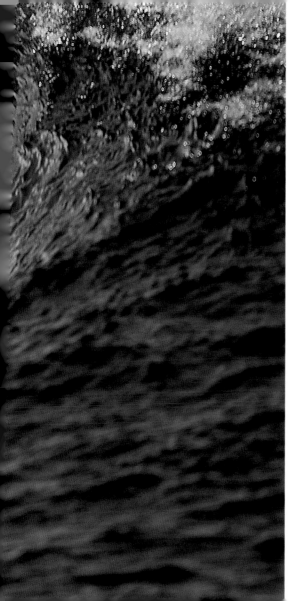

554-555 • America's Andy Irons masters the waves in Tahiti during the quarterfinals of the World Tour pro 2008 competition.

555 • Australian surfer Layne Beachley climbs the crest of a wave in Torquay.

556 • An aerial movement by a snowboard competitor on an artificial piste in London on October 25, 2008.

557 • Switzerland's Manuela Müller executing a back-flip in the aerials qualifiers at the freestyle skiing World Cup 2008-09 in Park City, Utah.

558 • Switzerland's Manuela Müller in the aerials qualifiers at the freestyle skiing
World Cup 2008-09 in Park City, Utah.

559 • America's Colby West in an 'X' during the finals of the halfpipe at the freestyle
skiing World Cup 2008-09 in Park City.

560 • China's Nina Li training before the aerials competition at the freestyle skiing World Cup 2008-09 in Park City.

561 • American Lacy Schnoor training before the aerial competition at the freestyle skiing World Cup 2008-09 in Park City.

562 ● France's Guilbaut Colas during the mogul competition at Vancouver's freestyle ski Grand Prix on February 7, 2009.

563 ● Canada's Alexandre Bilodeau in the final of the mogul competition at Vancouver's freestyle ski Grand Prix on February 7, 2009.

America's Michael Goldschmidt during the halfpipe of the Alli Dew Tour 2009 in Truckee, California.

Americans Lindsey Jacobellis, Sandra Frei and Olivia Nobs (from left) in flight during the boardercross competition of the 2008 snowboard World Cup in Gujo/Gifu, Japan.

Switzerland's Evelyn Leu performs a backflip in the aerials qualifiers at the freestyle skiing World Cup 2008-09 in Park City.

STRENGTH
POWER

and

Germany's Dirk Nowitzki dunks a basket during a game against Turkey in Group C of Eurobasket 2007, at Palma de Majorca. Germany won by 79 to 49.

INTRODUCTION Strength and Power

IN SPORT, AS IN LIFE, STRENGTH AND POWER ARE NOT NECESSARILY SYNONYMOUS. STRENGTH IS GENERALLY USED FOR COMBAT SPORTS, IN WHICH THE MATCH COMES DOWN, GIVEN AN EQUAL WEIGHT, TO THE PECULIARITIES OF THE ATHLETE'S CONSTITUTION. TWO BOXERS MAY HAVE THE SAME BUILD, BUT DIFFER SUBSTANTIALLY IN THE STRENGTH OF THEIR PUNCH.

"POWER" INSTEAD IS OFTEN USED WHEN TALKING OF THE INSTRUMENTS THAT THE SPORTSMAN EMPLOYS, SUCH AS AN ENGINE IN MOTOR RACES. POWER IS ALSO OFTEN USED AS A COLLECTIVE TERM: POWER IN A RUGBY SCRUM IS THE CAPACITY TO PUSH OVER ONE'S

America's Oluwafunmilayo "Funmi" Jimoh in flight at the 2008 Beijing Games.

INTRODUCTION Strength and Power

OPPONENTS, OR TO STOP THEM IN THEIR TRACKS.

THE TERMS ARE THEREFORE NOT NECESSARILY SYN-
ONYMOUS, EVEN THOUGH THEY ARE OFTEN COM-
BINED AND CONSIDERED AS SUCH. THEY CERTAINLY
ARE SYNONYMOUS THOUGH IN WEIGHTLIFTING, THE
SPORT THAT MEASURES STRENGTH MORE THAN ANY
OTHER. IT IS IN THIS CONTEXT THAT WE USUALLY LOOK
FOR 'THE STRONGEST MAN IN THE WORLD,' THE ONE
ABLE TO LIFT THE HEAVIEST WEIGHT AND ACCRUE THE
HIGHEST OVERALL TOTAL.

FEW WOULD TRY TO ARGUE THAT HOSSEIN REZA
ZADEH IS NOT THE STRONGEST MAN IN THE WORLD
TODAY, EVEN IF HIS ABSENCE FROM THE BEIJING
OLYMPICS, AFTER HIS DOUBLE GOLD IN 2000 AND

2004, OFFICIALLY DUE TO HIS BEING BANNED FROM COMPETITION BY HIS DOCTORS AFTER ACCIDENT, HAS BEEN THE SUBJECT OF SPECULATION ABOUT DOPING. HOSSEIN WAS BORN IN 1988 IN NORTHERN IRAN, IN ARDABIL, AN AFGHAN BORDER TOWN ON THE CASPIAN SEA. HE HAS BEEN DUBBED 'THE PERSIAN HERCULES.' HE DEBUTED AS A WEIGHTLIFTER AT 15 YEARS OF AGE. TWO YEARS LATER HE ASTONISHED THE WORLD WINNING THE GOLD MEDAL AT THE SYDNEY OLYMPICS, THE FIRST NON-SOVIET OR NON-RUSSIAN LIFTER TO DO SO IN 40 YEARS, WITH A WORLD RECORD TOTAL OF 472.5 KG (1041.6 LBS). THIS WAS VERY CLOSE TO THE MAGIC TARGET OF 500 KG (1102.3 LBS) THAT HOSSEIN, HOWEVER, HAS NEVER REACHED.

Strength and Power

Introduction

A VERY RELIGIOUS MAN, HOSSEIN USUALLY SAYS A PRAYER BEFORE LIFTING THE BAR AND HE RELAXES BY LISTENING TO MUSIC. HE IS A LEGENDARY FIGURE IN IRAN. ARDABIL'S SPORTS CENTER IS NAMED AFTER HIM, AS IS A BANK. THE IRANIAN PRESIDENT HAS EVEN DONATED 600 MILLION RIALS (ABOUT $70,000) TO HIM SO THAT HE CAN BUILD A HOUSE IN TEHERAN. HOSSEIN'S WEDDING WAS BROADCAST PRIME TIME AND LIVE ON TV FROM MECCA THROUGHOUT THE COUNTRY.

● The strength of superman Michael Phelps during the butterfly leg of the 400 meter medley at the 2007 World Swimming Championships in Melbourne, where he broke five world records and won seven gold medals.

578 ● Germany's Fabian Hambüchen during the vault in the team final at the 2007 World Gymnastics Championships in Stuttgart.

579 ● Vault by Japan's Hisashi Mizutori, in the individual final at the 2007 World Gymnastic Championships in Stuttgart.

580 ● Alexander Artemev, of Belorussian origin but competing for the USA where he has lived since he was nine, on the pommel horse at the 2008 Beijing Games. He fell during the exercise, finishing seventh in the equipment final.

580-581 ● One-handed vault on the pommel horse for Japan's Hiroyuki Tomita, competing at the 2008 Beijing Games in the individual final of the all-round competition in which he finished fourth.

582 • An aerial vault on the rings by America's David Durante at the USA 2008 Olympic trials in Philadelphia.

583 • Maneuver on the rings for Australia's Philippe Rizzo in the team competition at the 2006 Commonwealth Games in Melbourne. Australia won silver behind Canada and Rizzo came eighth in the individual competition.

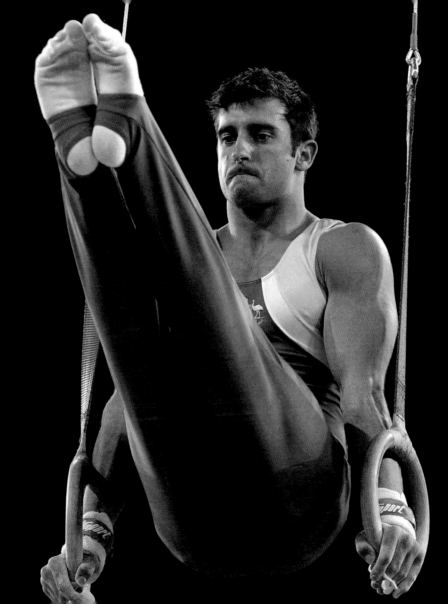

584-585 • China's Huang Xu in flight on the rings in the qualifiers for the equipment competition in the 2008 Beijing Games. Huang won the team gold, but was immediately eliminated on the rings.

585 • A gymnast's iron grip on the rings during the individual competition at the 2008 Beijing Games.

Sheffield Wednesday
goalkeeper Lee Grant
dives to save a free kick
from Wigan's Daniel De
Ridder in a pre-season
friendly played
in Sheffield on
August 2, 2008.

588 • Grabbed by the leg, Ma'a Nonu of the All Blacks stops running in a 2008 Tri Nations match against Australia in Brisbane.

589 • Inter Milan's Balotelli tries to intercept a pass, under pressure from Torino's Di Loreto. Inter went on to win 1-0 with a goal by Cruz after 30 minutes.

590 • Final qualification match in the Australian Rugby League Championship, in Sydney on September 12, 2008. James Aubusson of the Roosters runs with the ball towards the Broncos' line.

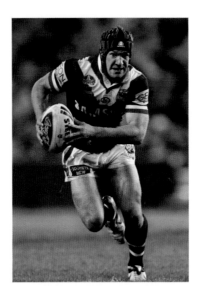

591 • Brandon Jacobs of the New York Giants starts to run with the ball towards the New England Patriots' goal line in an NFL home game, won by the Patriots by 38-35.

592 ● Line-out in the England-Italy match in rugby's Six Nations at Twickenham on February 10, 2007: England's Danny Grewcock and Magnus Lund fight for the ball with Italy's Marco Bortolami.

592-593 ● Israel Folau of Queensland grabs the ball and scores during the third State of Origin rugby league match against New South Wales Blues on July 2, 2008 in Sydney.

America's Natalie Coughlin in action in the closing stage of the of the final of the 200 meter medley at the 2008 Beijing Games, in which she won bronze.

596 • Start of the final of the 200 meter backstroke at the 2008 Beijing Games. From top are winner Kirsty Coventry from Zimbabwe, Australian Meagen Nay, seventh, and American Margaret Hoelzer, second.

597 • The start of the final of the 100 meter backstroke at the Australian Youth Olympic Festival in Sydney on January 15, 2009.

598-599 • America's Michael Phelps in the butterfly stage of the semifinal of the 200 meter medley at the 2008 Beijing Games.

600-601 • Michael Phelps, USA, in the butterfly heats of the 2008 Beijing Games, one of the eight events in which he competed at the Olympics.

602-603 • Austria's Helmut Oblinger in action in a K1 slalom heat during the kayak races at the 2008 Beijing Games.

603 • Japan's Takuya Haneda during the C1 canoe single heats at the 2008 Beijing Games.

604 ● Sweden's Isak Ohrstrom during a heat of the K1 slalom at the 2008 Beijing Games.

604-605 ● Italian duo of Erik Masoero and Andrea Benetti in the final of the C2 slalom at the 2008 Beijing Games. The Italian team went on to finish fifth.

606 • Russia's Marat Safin serving against Switzerland's Roger Federer in the third round of the 2007 Wimbledon Singles. Federer won the match in three sets.

607 • A strange expression on the face of Rafael Nadal, serving against Russia's Mikhail Yuzhny in the quarterfinals of the 2008 Wimbledon singles competition.

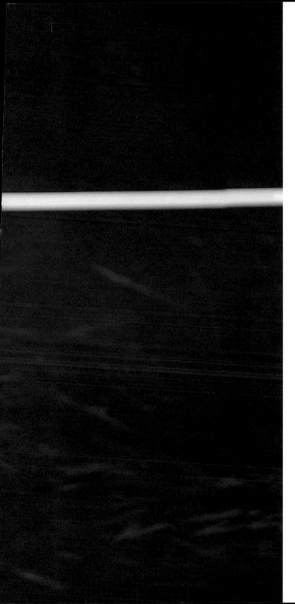

608-609 • America's Sam Warburg serving against Serb Dusan Vemic at the 2008 Los Angeles Countryside Classic.

609 • Switzerland's Roger Federer serving against Russia's Marat Safin at Wimbledon 2007.

610-611 • Venus Williams returns with a powerful drive in the quarterfinals of the 2008 Wimbledon singles against Thailand's Tamarine Tanasugarn.

611 • Serena Williams, USA, serves against Pole Urszula Radwanskai in the second round of the 2008 Wimbledon singles.

612 • Maria Sharapova serves in the second round of Wimbledon 2007 against France's Severine Bremond.

612-613 • Sharapova serves at Wimbledon during the first round of the 2008 tournament against France's Stephanie Foretz.

614 • Australian Eliza Hynes dives for a catch at the Australian Youth Olympic Festival in Sydney in January of 2009.

615 • Dahammaka Rohan Silva Gajasingha Badana Arachige of Sri Lanka serves against the Kazakh pair in the 2008 Asian Games in Bali.

616 • US long-jumper Miguel Pate in mid-air during the ISTAF meeting in Berlin in 2008.

616-617 • A bad landing on her back in the sand for Nigerian Blessing Okagbare in the long-jump qualifiers at the 2008 Beijing Games. Okagbare just managed to qualify for the final, in which she won the bronze medal.

618 • US decathlete Brian Clay in the high jump at the 2008 US Olympic trials at Eugene, Oregon.

619 • American heptathlete Jacquelyn Johnson hits the bar in the decathlon high jump at the 2008 US Olympic trials at Eugene, Oregon.

620 • Belgium's Hans van Alphen during the decathlon shot put at the 2008 US Olympic trials at Eugene.

621 • America's Rhuben Williams in the shot put at the 2008 US Olympic trials at Eugene, in which he finished tenth.

622 • France's Antoinette Nana Djimou Ida in the heptathlon shot put at the 2008 Beijing Games.

623 • Germany's Michael Schrader throws the discus during the decathlon at the 2008 Beijing Games, where he finished tenth.

624 • With minimal clothing, Byelorussia's Yana Maksimova is about to throw the javelin during the heptathlon at the 2008 Beijing Games, in which she finished last.

624-625 • China's Lingwei Li hurls her javelin in the qualifiers for the 2006 Junior World Championships in Beijing. She finished eighth in the final.

626 • Run-up in the javelin by Germany's Christina Obergföll during the 2007 World Athletics Championships in Osaka that saw her win the silver.

626-627 • The Czech Republic's Barbora Spotakova throws during the qualifiers for the 2008 Beijing Games: Spotakova went on to win the gold in the final.

628 • Cuba's Guillermo Martinez in action in the javelin qualifiers at the 2007 World Athletics Championships in Osaka. He finished ninth in the final.

629 • Cincinnati Reds pitcher Johnny Cueto in action in the against the Tampa Bay Rays in a 2008 pre-season game in Sarasota.

• Ryan Zimmermann of the Washington Nationals hits a home run in the ninth inning against the Atlanta Braves on March 30, 2008. The Nationals won 3-2.

632-633 • Slovakia's Ivan Batory is pursued closely by Italy's Fulvio Valbusa at the start of the 50 km cross country ski race at the 2006 Turin Winter Olympics in Pragelato, on February 26, 2006. Valbusa finished 30th and Batory 47th.

633 • The Czech Republic's Katerina Neumannova is about to win the 10 km free at the 2007 Nordic World Ski Championships in Saporo.

634 • At the 2007 Pan American
Games in Rio de Janeiro,
Salvadorian weightlifter Eva Dimas
shows her satisfaction
with a successful clean and jerk
in the 75 kg class.

634-635 • America's Amanda
Hubbard is about to complete her
attempt in the weightlifting at the
2008 US Olympic trials in Atlanta.

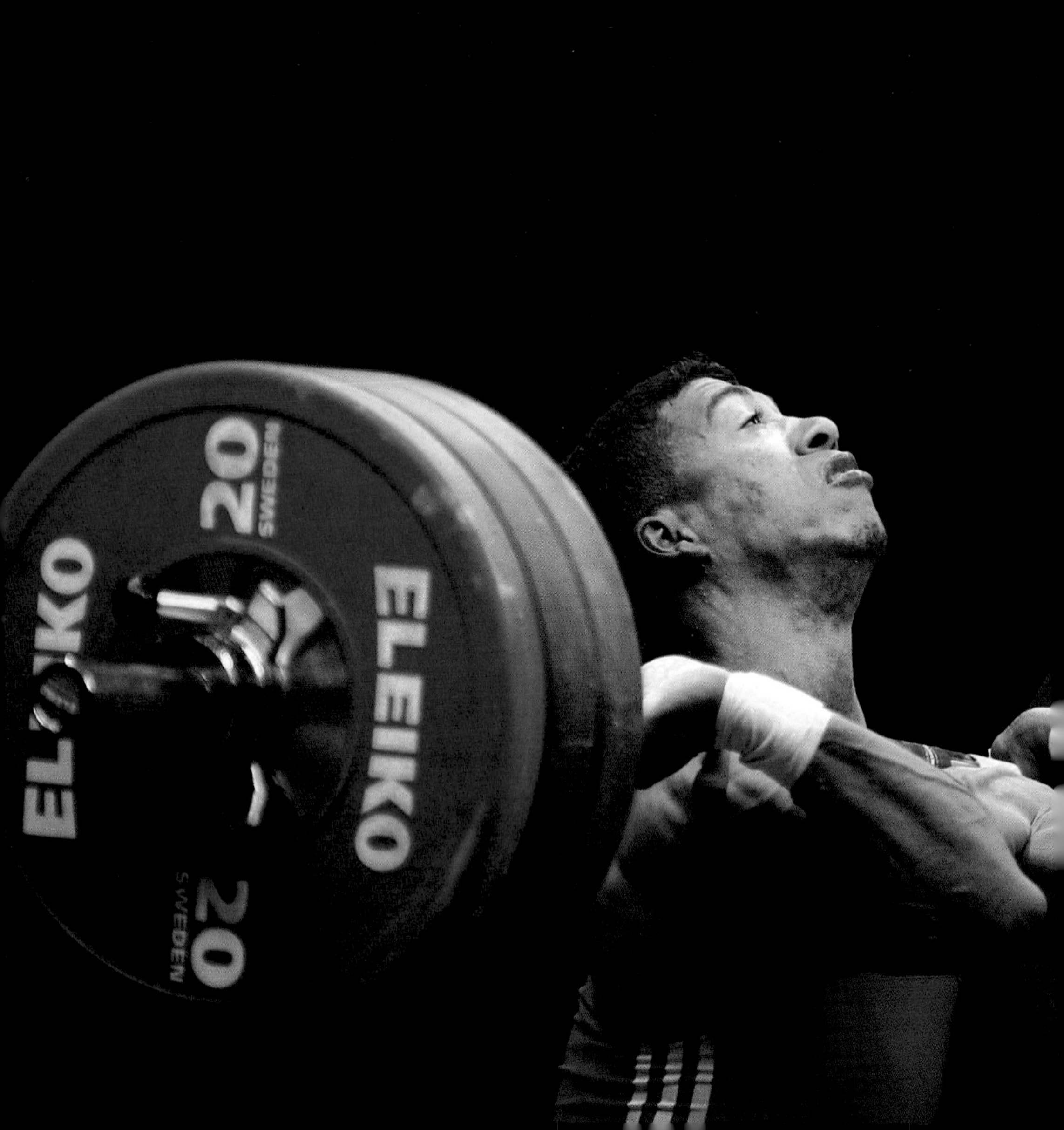
20
SWEDEN
ELEIKO
20
SWEDEN

636-637 • Colombia's Diego Salazar in the 63 kg clean and jerk at the 2007 Pan American Games in Rio de Janeiro, in which she won the gold medal.

637 • American Jason Starks starts to exert his strength in the snatch at the 2008 US Olympic weightlifting trials.

MAN against MAN

- De Shawn Wynn, the Green Bay Packers' running back, is gripped by five New York Giants defenders, in an NFL match in East Rutherford, New Jersey, on September 16, 2007.

INTRODUCTION Main Against Man

LEADING SOCIOLOGISTS IN THEORIZING ABOUT THE ANALOGY BETWEEN THE ACTIONS AND SYMBOLISM OF SPORT AND WAR ARGUE THAT THE PHYSICAL CONTEST CARRIES SOME OF THE FLAVOR OF BATTLE, OF ARMED CONFLICTS BETWEEN COUNTRIES AND COMMUNITIES. OF COURSE THEY ARE RIGHT TO SAY THAT THE RITUAL ORIGIN OF SPORT IS ROOTED IN THE TRANSPOSITION OF VIOLENT WARLIKE CLASHES INTO BLOODLESS COMPETITION.

HOWEVER THE PHYSICAL CLASH IN SPORT HAS BEEN OR SHOULD BE ABOUT THE AFFIRMATION OF SUPERIORITY WITHIN PARTICULAR SET RULES, IN A FAIR FIGHT

• Russia's Rakhim Chakhkiev (red vest) against Italy's Clemente Russo in the heavyweight final at the 2008 Beijing Games, which Chakhkiev won on points.

INTRODUCTION Main Against Man

IN WHICH THE AIM IS TO OVERCOME THE RIVAL VIA THE LEGITIMATE AND ACCEPTED MEANS OF SPORTING COMPETITION. INDEED, THIS SORT OF VIOLENCE IS CENTRAL TO COMBAT SPORTS: KNOCKING OVER ONE'S OPPONENT WITH A VIOLENT THRUST OF THE ARM IS THE STUFF OF BOXING HALLS, WRESTLING AND FENCING. THIS IS THE CASE EVEN THOUGH SPORT ESSENTIALLY SEEKS TO REDUCE THE LEVEL OF DANGER TO THAT OF A SIMPLE, ACCEPTABLE DEFEAT.

SINCE ANTIQUITY, WHEN TOURNAMENTS TO FIND THE STRONGEST, THE MOST ABLE OR THE MOST CUNNING TOOK PLACE AT THE SAME TIME AS PARTIES, CELEBRATIONS OR TRIBUTES TO THE GODS, THE PRINCIPLES OF CORRECTNESS AND FAIR PLAY HAVE BEEN JEALOUSLY

INTRODUCTION Main Against Man

GUARDED. THE PHYSICAL CLASH IS SUBLIMATED BY THE FINAL HUG BETWEEN VICTOR AND VANQUISHED.

HOWEVER THERE WERE SOME VERY RARE EXCEPTIONS. ANCIENT HISTORIANS RECORDED A VERY FAMOUS ONE. IT TOOK PLACE ON THE PLAIN OF OLYMPIA, WHERE THE GAMES IN HONOR OF ZEUS WERE HELD DURING THE WHOLE OF THE FIRST MILLENNIUM B.C. AND FOR A FURTHER 400 YEARS AFTERWARD. WE KNOW FOR SURE THAT IT HAPPENED IN 564 B.C., WHEN FOR THE THIRD CONSECUTIVE TIME, ARRACHION OF PHIGALIA, TWICE OLYMPIC CHAMPION, REACHED THE FINAL OF THE PANCRATIUM, A BRUTAL MIX OF BOXING AND WRESTLING. CAUGHT BY HIS RIVAL IN A STRANGULATION GRIP, ARRACHION TRIED TO TRIED TO FREE

Man Against Man

Introduction

HIMSELF WHILE HE WAS BEING SUFFOCATED AND MANAGED TO SHIFT HIS OPPONENT'S LEG, DISLOCATING THE MAN'S ANKLE VERY BADLY. IN FALLING AND LETTING GO OF HIS GRIP, HIS RIVAL RAISED A FINGER IN SIGN OF SURRENDER AND THE JUDGES IMMEDIATELY DECLARED ARRACHION THE WINNER. IT WAS A SHAME THAT IN THE MEANTIME HE HAD DIED FROM A BROKEN NECK.... THAT TIME PHYSICAL SPORTS COMBAT CLAIMED A LIFE AND IT DID SO AT THE HANDS OF THE DEFEATED PARTY.

● Argentina's Manu Ginobili (black vest, San Antonio Spurs) and Jannero Pargo of the New Orleans Hornets dive on a disputed ball in game one of the 2008 NBA playoffs in New Orleans.

646 • Caught between Brodney Pool and Terry Cousin of the Cleveland Browns, Hines Ward of the Pittsburgh Steelers fails to find an opening and loses the ball during an NFL game in Cleveland on September 14, 2008.

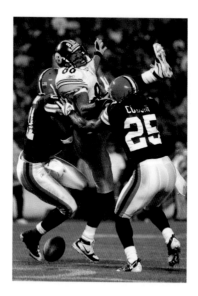

647 • The Nevada Wolf Pack attack is met by the Missouri Tigers' defense during the first period of the game at the Memorial Stadium in Colombia, Missouri.

648 • Plaxico Burress of the NY Giants grabs the mask of his opponent, Ronde Barber of the Tampa Bay Buccaneers to hold off a block.

649 • Despite the efforts of Richard Marshall of the Carolina Panthers (left) Tony Gonzales of the Kansas City Chiefs makes his 102nd reception, an NFL record, in Charlotte on October 5, 2008.

650 ● Cecil Sapp of the Denver Broncos, in the center wearing 27, is blocked as he dives towards the line by the San Diego Chargers' defense at San Diego on December 24, 2007.

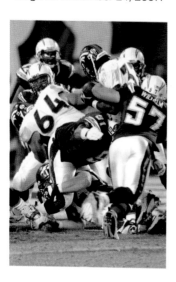

650-651 ● Collective defensive block by the Missouri Tigers to stop the progress of Via Taua of the Nevada Wolf Pack, during a game at Columbia (Missouri).

652 • Buffalo Bills quarterback Trent Edwards tries to escape the Philadelphia Eagles' defense in December of 2007.

652-653 • New York Jets quarterback, Brett Favre, in white, is caught by New England Patriots' defenders in a 2008 NFL game at East Rutherford, which the Patriots went on to win 19-10.

654 • Bryan Thomas and Calvin Pace of the NY Jets block Chad Pennington of the Miami Dolphins in a 2008-2009 NFL game in Miami.

654-655 • There was nothing that Navy Midshipmen quarterback Jarod Bryant could do when blocked by the Duke Blue Devils defense in this 2008-09 season college game in Durham.

656 ● China's Xuang Han (in blue) tries to prevent a hold by South Korea's Min Sun Aea during the 2007 China Judo Open in Beijing.

657 ● Austria's Ludwig Paischer (left) faces Moroccan Youned Ahmadi in the 60 kg preliminary judo rounds at the 2008 Beijing Games.

658 • A hold by Israeli Gal Yekutiel (blue) against Britain's Craig Fallon in the repechage of the 60 kg judo tournament at the 2008 Beijing Games.

658-659 • A leg hold by American Taraje Williams-Murray against Japan's Hiroaki Hiraokad during the preliminary rounds of the 60 kg judo tournament at the 2008 Beijing Games. The American won 1-0.

660 • Cuba's Anaysi Hernandez (back) celebrates her success against German Annett Böhmi in the final bout of the second round of the 70 kg judo at the 2008 Beijing Games.

661 • Spain's Esther San Miguel and Russia's Vyera Moskalyuk face each other in the preliminary round of the 78 kg judo tournament at the 2008 Beijing Games.

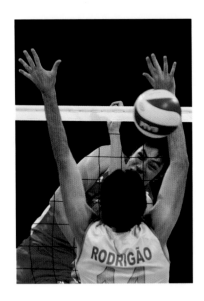

662 ● A goal by China's Yu Dawei beats the block by Brazilian Anderson Rodrigues in the volleyball match between the two countries at the 2008 Beijing Games.

663 ● Holland's Kay van Dijk about to overcome the American wall during the final of the San Diego volleyball tournament, at the Jenny Craig Pavilion on June 12, 2005.

Brazil's Marianne Steinbrecher (number 3) tries to force through the wall of three American opponents during the volleyball final at the 2008 Beijing Games.

666 ● American David Lee (blue) blocks Serbia's Novica Bjelica during the volleyball match between the USA and Serbia at the 2008 Beijing Games.

666-667 ● Italy's wall, made up of Matteo Martino, Luigi Mastrangelo and Valerio Vermiglio tries to stop Russian Alexander Kosaryov's spike during the Italy-Russia volleyball match for the bronze medal at the 2008 Beijing Games.

668-669 • Puerto Rican McWilliams Arroyo Acevedo dodges a right by Cuban Andris Laffita Hernandez in the 51 kg boxing quarterfinal at the 2008 Beijing Games.

670-671 • Great Britain's James DeGale dodges Cuban Emilio Correa Bayeaux (in blue) during the final of the 75 kg boxing at the 2008 Beijing Games, which the Cuban went on to win.

672 • American Tim Bradley hits the face of Britain's Junior Witter with a left jab during the World Junior Welterweight boxing match in Nottingham in 2008, in which the American won the crown.

673 • America's Qa'id Muhammad, known as Kid Dynamite (left), tries to get behind the guard of Mexico's Samuel Gutierrez during his third professional bantamweight fight, in Atlantic City in October of 2008, which he went on to win by a knockout.

Japan's Crazy Kim (real name Toshiharu Kaneyama) faces Australia's Anthony Mundine, the eventual winner, in a non-title Super Middleweight fight in Newcastle, Australia in 2008. Above, Crazy Kim hits his opponent, who goes down (right).

676 • A tough tackle by Newcastle United's Geremi on Tottenham's Assou-Ekotto in a 2008 League Cup match, in Newcastle, England.

676-677 • A blatant foul by Hummels on Kuranyi of Schalke in a 2008-09 Bundesliga season match in Dortmund.

678 • Bologna-Roma, Serie A, November 8, 2008: Francesco Totti jumps over an opponent to avoid a foul.

679 • In challenging for a high ball, Arsenal's Adebayor sticks an elbow in the face of Hull City's Shane, whose team-mate Michael Turner looks worried as he helps him on the ground, during a 2008-09 season game at Arsenal's Emirates Stadium.

● An unsuccessful dive by Manchester City goalkeeper Hart while Liverpool's Kuyt scores the decisive goal between the two teams in a 2008-09 Premier League match in Manchester.

682-683 ● Italy's Luca Ansoldi knocks down Russia's Alexander Yeremyenko during the preliminary stage match of the 2008 World Ice Hockey Championships in Québec City in Canada.

683 ● Russia's Andrey Kovalyenko prepares to take a penalty against Swiss goalkeeper Renato Tosio in a Victoria Cup match in Berne.

684 • A battle for the puck between Germans Ullman and Osterloh (white jersey) and Norway's Hansen in the preliminary stage match at the 2007 World Ice Hockey Championships in Moscow.

685 • Markus Naslund of the New York Rangers is about to squeeze Metallurg Magnitogorsk's Alexander Seluyanov in a body check during a 2008 Victoria Cup game in Berne.

686 • Yann Danis of the NY Islanders gets in the way of a shot by Bobby Ryan of the Anaheim Ducks in a 2008-09 NHL match in Uniondale.

687 • World Championships Final in Québec City: Russia's Nabokov intercepts the puck that has escaped goalkeeper Proshkin after he saved a shot by the Canadian Tows (left). Russia went on to win the title 5-4 in extra time.

688 • Welsh players tackle France's Serge Betsen during the France-Wales rugby match at the 2007 Six Nations in Paris.

689 • Anthony Quinn of the Melbourne Storm emerges from a scrum with the ball in an Australian Rugby League game against the Parramatta Eels in 2007.

690-691 • Peter Saili of Auckland is blocked by Api Naikatini of Wellington in a 2008 Air New Zealand Cup rugby match in Auckland.

691 • He has won the ball but Israel Folau of the Melbourne Storm is about to be blocked by the Cowboys during this 2007-08 Australian Rugby League match.

England's Harry Ellis takes the ball from his markers and opens up despite being tackled by Ireland's Peter Stringer in a 2006-07 Six Nations match in Dublin.

694 • Wales's Shane Williams is literally carried off by England's Vainikolo and Bailshaw in the 2007-08 Six Nations rugby match at Twickenham.

695 • Italy's Mirco Bergamasco is tackled by the Welsh defense during a 2007-08 Six Nations rugby match in Cardiff.

696 • Tri Nations 2008: Australia rugby player Berrick Barnes is tackled during the match against the All Blacks in Sydney.

697 • Australia's James Horville shouts in celebration after a try during the same Tri Nations match. Australia won 34-19, but New Zealand went on to win the tournament.

688-689 • Justin Morneau (right) of the Minnesota Twins pre-empts the arrival at base of Brian McCann of the Atlanta Braves in the Major League All Star Game, to win 4-3 at Yankee Stadium.

699 • Ben Zobrist (Tampa Bay) is beaten to the base by Omir Santos (63, Baltimore Orioles) in a 2008 Major League match in Baltimore.

700 • Chris Kroski (Cincinnati Reds, ground) beats David Eckstein (Toronto Blue Jays) to the base during a pre-season match at Sarasota in March, 2008.

701 • Toronto Marlins second base Chris Coghlan (in the air) completes a double play, despite the desperate dive by Troy Glaus of the St. Louis Cardinals in a 2008 pre-season match in Jupiter, Florida.

702 ● Pablo Ozuna of the Chicago White Sox beats Conor Jackson of the Arizona Diamondbacks to the base in a 2008 pre-season game in Tucson, Arizona.

702-703 ● Second baseman Marcus Giles of the Colorado Rockies performs a double play despite the desperate slide by Mark Reynolds of the Arizona Diamondbacks in a 2008 pre-season game in Tucson.

A loose ball is bitterly contested by Solomon Tat of the Virginia Cavaliers (left) and Kyle Singles of the Duke Blue Devils in the NBA 2007-2008 season match in Durham, North Carolina, won by Duke 87-65.

706 • Shooting, Brandon Roy (white jersey) of the Portland Trail Blazers tries to avoid being stopped by Yao Ming of the Houston Rockets in a 2008-09 NBA match in Portland.

707 • Avoiding the Cleveland Cavaliers defense, Louis Williams of the Philadelphia 49ers goes undisturbed to the basket in the NBA 2007-08 season match in Philadelphia.

708 ● A struggle on the bounce between the Minnesota Lynx defense and Sanford (first to the ball) and Gardner of the Washington Mystics in Minneapolis on August 30, 2008.

709 ● Jumping to catch the ball on the rebound are American Candace Parker and Russia's Maria Styepanova (right) at the 2008 Beijing Games.

710 • A Swede of Turkish-Armenian origin, Ara Abrahamian grabs his French rival Mélonin Noumonvi in the 84 kg Greco-Roman wrestling match at the 2008 Beijing Games. He won the bronze medal but it was later revoked because he left the podium during the ceremony.

711 • Turkey's Soner Sucu and Cuba's Roberto Monzon look for a hold in the 60 kg Greco-Roman wrestling repechage at the 2008 Beijing Games.

712 • Nepal's Ram Limbu (red belt) tries to strike Tajik Aligon Sarimasqov in the 55 kg kumite match at the 2006 Asian Karate Games in Doha, Qatar.

713 • In the repechage for the final round of the 60 kg kumite at the 2007 Asian Games in Doha, Abdullah Dallol of Qatar (red belt) scores a hit against his opponent, Nguyen Ngoc Thanh of Vietnam.

• Two moments in the bout between Japan's Yuki Ota (red stripes) and Benjamin Philip Kleibrink (Germany) in the final of the individual foil in the 2008 Beijing Games, won by the German.

716 ● Roberto Bertinetti, young Italian fencing promise, carrying out an attack during the 2008 Bertinetti Trophy.

717 ● Valentina Vezzali (right) and Margherita Granbassi meet in the final heat of the individual foil at the 2008 Beijing Games. Vezzali won gold and Granbassi bronze.

718-719 ● Venezuela's Ruben Limardo (left) fights Cuba's Andrea Carrillo, the eventual winner, in the individual saber final of the 2007 Pan American Games in Rio de Janeiro.

720 • China's Liang Zhongxing tries to stop Greece's Georgios Afroudakis from reaching the ball in the water polo quarterfinal at the 2008 Beijing Games.

720-721 • Younger brother of Afroudakis, Christos, from behind, tries not to be beaten to the ball by Canada's Thomas Marks in the victorious first round water polo match at the 2008 Beijing Games.

722 • Hungary's Norbert Hosnyanszky goes to shoot, opposed by a Canadian defender in the preliminary water polo match at the 2008 Beijing Games

723 • Serbia's Andrija Prlainovic and Nikola Radijen try to stop Montenegro's Boris Zlokovic from recovering the ball in the water polo final group match, won by Serbia 6-4, at the 2008 Beijing Games.

Sweden's Markus Oscarsson (in the foreground) in the semifinal of the K1 100 meter kayak race at the 2008 Beijing Games, winning a place in the final where he finished sixth.

● Final of the women's
K2 500 meters at the
2008 Beijing Games; in
the foreground are
Hungary's Katalin
Kovacs and Natasa
Janic, who have a
narrow lead over the
Poles Beata Mikolajczyk
and Aneta Pastuszka-
Konieczna, whom they
beat by 0.784 seconds.

Valeria Manferto De Fabianis is the editor of the series.
She was born in Vercelli, Italy and studied arts at the Università Cattolica del Sacro Cuore in Milan, graduating with a degree in philosophy. She is an enthusiastic traveler and nature lover. She has collaborated on the production of television documentaries and articles for the most prestigious Italian specialty magazines and has also written many photography books. She co-founded Edizioni White Star in 1984 with Marcello Bertinetti and is the editorial director.

INDEX

ALL PHOTOGRAPHS ARE BY GETTY IMAGES

A special thank you to Max Giannotta

Text by **Elio Trifari**: born in Naples on 17 March 1945, married with one daughter; an electronic engineering graduate, who has lived in Milan since 1973, where, after five years as a freelance covering track and field events, he joined Gazzetta dello Sport, where he still works. Here he became deputy chief of Olympic sports, chief writer and deputy editor and edited the Gazzetta weekly magazine from 1995 to 2000. In 1984 he published a three volume 'History of the Olympics' for Rizzoli. In 2006 he coordinated the 31 volumes of '110 years of glory', the history of sport via the pages of Gazzetta dello Sport. In 2008 he published an 'Olympic Encyclopedia', two volumes in Italian and one in English. Then in 2009 he and Pier Bergonzi compiled the official book for the Centenary of the Giro d'Italia. All these works were released by Gazzetta.

Cover ● From left:
first row - Patrice Evra (France) and Mauro Camoranesi (Italy); Alberto Contador (Spain);
Jean-Baptiste Grange (France).
second row - Michael Phelps (USA); Serena Williams (USA); Rozle Prezelj (Slovenia).
third row - Shin Sooji (South Korea); the German pursuit team;
Benjamin Darbelet (France) and Rachid Rguig (Morocco).

● Tanith Belbin and Benjamin Agosto (USA) in the free dance
at the Grand Prix ISU-Cup of China 2008.

Back cover ● From left:
first row - Camilo Villegas (Colombia); Ervin Santana (Dominican Republic); Carolina Kostner (Italy).
second row - Patrick Cobbs (USA); Louis Williams (USA); Torri Edwards (USA).
third row - Felipe Massa (Brazil); Sven Ruenow (Australia); Benjamin Philip Kleibrink (Germany)
and Yuki Ota (Japan).